NEW YORK
Off the Beaten Path

"Journeying into corners of New York unknown to many natives, William Scheller reveals a state rich in history and geography that always has something new to offer travelers and adventure seekers."
  —*Press Republican,* Plattsburgh

"This is a book not only for those visiting the Empire State but for natives as well. . . . As Scheller points out over and over there is plenty to see once a traveler turns off the main road."
  —*The Oneida* (NY) *Dispatch*

"An easygoing guidebook to the unusual . . . these pages can inspire a day's drive or a weekend trip."
  —*Ridgewood* (NY) *Times*

"For all those people who don't always have the desire to hike and canoe every moment of their free time, this handy paperback is the answer . . . a good addition for anyone who enjoys exploring places that are "off the beaten path."
  —*Adirondack Mountain Club* newsletter

NEW YORK
Off the Beaten Path

Second Edition

by **William G. Scheller**

A Voyager Book

Chester, Connecticut

This book is for Kay.

Library of Congress Cataloging-in-Publication Data

Scheller, William.
   New York: off the beaten path / William G. Scheller. — 2nd ed.
     p. cm.
   "A Voyager book."
   ISBN 0-87106-620-3
    1. New York (State)—Description and travel—1981- —Guide-books.
 I. Title.
 F119.3.S34 1990
 917.4704'43—dc20

89-48810
CIP

Illustrations by Steve Baldwin

Manufactured in the United States of America
Second Edition/Second Printing

Contents

Introduction vii

East of the Hudson 1

The Adirondacks 25

The Mohawk Valley 49

The Southern Tier 71

The Lakeshore 91

The Catskills 105

New York City and Long Island 117

Index 142

New York

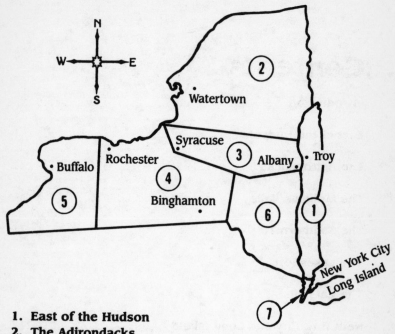

1. **East of the Hudson**
2. **The Adirondacks**
3. **The Mohawk Valley**
4. **The Southern Tier**
5. **The Lakeshore**
6. **The Catskills**
7. **New York City and Long Island**

Introduction

At first glance, there would appear to be one overriding problem with fitting a state like New York into the "Off the Beaten Path" series of travel books: The paths that run between Montauk and Niagara, between Binghamton and Massena, are among the most heavily beaten in the United States. The Dutch were in lower Manhattan before the Pilgrims landed at Plymouth; the population of New York State was only eclipsed by that of California within the past twenty years. Could there be any stones left unturned in such a place, any byways not trod so often as to become commonplace?

Yes, there are—precisely because of the long history of New York and the many millions of people who have lived and worked there. New York occupies a unique position in American history, a position between that of the small, densely settled New England states and the western expanses left untamed well into the nineteenth century. With the exception of the Dutch settlements at New Amsterdam and along the Hudson Valley, New York remained a virtual frontier until the late 1700s. When it was settled the newcomers were not colonists from abroad but in many cases migrating New Englanders, men and women setting the pattern for the next hundred years of westward expansion. New York thus became a transitional place between old, coastal America and the horizons of the West.

More than that, the future "Empire State" became a staging area for the people, ideas, and physical changes that would transform the United States in the nineteenth century. Its position between the harbors of the Atlantic coast and the Great Lakes assured early prominence in the development of canals and later railroads. Its vast resources made it an industrial power, while its size and fertility guaranteed its importance as a farm state. It began its growth early enough to create an infrastructure of small towns connected by back roads, rivers, and canals and remained vigorous in a modern era conducive to the rise of great cities along busy trunk-line railroads. All the while, the state's geographical diversity allowed its different regions to assume varied and distinct personalities.

The spiritual and intellectual atmosphere in New York was no less responsive to change. This is where the quietist Shakers played out much of their experiment in plain living. It's also where a young man named Joseph Smith announced that he had been shown lost books of the Bible proclaiming God's mission in the New World, and founded Mormonism. The nineteenth-century fascination with spiritualism flourished in New York State, as did the early pop-culture phenomenon known as Chautauqua. Washington Irving proclaimed a native American literature here, and the artists of the Hudson River School painted American nature as it had never been painted before. When the English Arts and Crafts movement arrived in the United States at the end of the last century, one of its principal beachheads was at the studios of Elbert Hubbard in East Aurora, New York.

This book is about the rich legacy of tangible associations that all of this activity has left behind. New York is crammed as are few other states with the homes, libraries, and workshops of famous individuals, with battlefields and the remnants of historic canals, with museums chronicling pursuits as divergent as horse racing, glassblowing, gunsmithing, and winemaking. In a place where people have done just about everything, here are reminders of just about everything they've ever done. And while some of the destinations listed here regularly find their way into conventional guidebooks, most are hidden among the placid backwaters of the state. New York has no shortage of small and middle-size towns easily overlooked by superhighway travelers, and unlike many of the pretty villages of nearby New England, they have remained uncommercialized and very unselfconscious. An exploration of the New York State countryside will reveal dozens upon dozens of these communities and their attractions, along with miles of lush farmland and undisturbed natural surroundings.

The sheer size of New York State makes a system of geographic subdivision necessary in a book with upwards of 130 individual listings. I have thus drawn a new set of boundaries within New York (see map), defining seven distinct territories: East of the Hudson; the Adirondacks; the Mohawk Valley; the Southern Tier; the Lakeshore; the Catskills; and New York City and Long Island. As much as possible, these boundaries have been drawn to reflect the natural distinctions that divide one area from another; however, a small number of arbitrary decisions were unavoidable. If you occasionally disagree, and would rather see Saratoga clustered with the Mohawk Valley than with the Adirondacks, just ignore my designation. You won't need a visa to hop from one chapter to another.

Within each chapter, the order of individual listings has been determined geographically, as explained in the chapter introductions. Few readers will be proceeding dutifully from site to site, so no attempt has been made to provide detailed linking directions. Still, it's nice to know what's near what if a slightly longer drive would make visits to several destinations possible.

And so, off to New York State. An especially enlightening journey is promised to all those New Englanders who thought the world ended at Lake Champlain; to Manhattanites for whom "Upstate" is *terra incognita;* to Midwesterners, Westerners, and Southerners who feel they hold the patents on small towns and open country; and to travelers from abroad who would like to learn a little more about how America came to be what it is.

The rest of you are from New York State, and you know what you've been hiding.

*   *   *

Note to Readers: In the course of writing this book, I was careful to obtain the most recent available information regarding schedules and admission fees at each attraction described. All of these details were accurate at the time the book went to press; however, hours of operation and price are always subject to change. Just to be sure, use the telephone numbers provided to check these details before each visit.

Off the Beaten Path East of the Hudson

1. The Hudson River Museum
2. Philipse Manor Hall
3. Thomas Paine Cottage and Museum
4. Museum of Cartoon Art
5. Lyndhurst
6. Sunnyside
7. John Jay Homestead
8. Caramoor
9. Southeast Museum
10. Boscobel
11. Van Wyck Homestead
12. Mills Mansion
13. Old Rhinebeck Aerodrome
14. Crailo Gardens
15. Clermont
16. Olana
17. Shaker Museum
18. Crailo
19. Rensselaer County Junior Museum
20. Bennington Battlefield
21. New Skete Communities

East of the Hudson

The first of our seven New York State regions begins in the crowded bedroom communities of Westchester County and extends northwards into the western foothills of the Berkshires and Green Mountains. Hilly itself throughout, it encompasses the eastern slopes of one of the most beautiful river valleys in the world. Anyone in need of convincing should drive north along the length of the Taconic State Parkway, which runs through the high country midway between the Hudson and the Connecticut and Massachusetts borders. Along with the more easterly and meandering State Route 22, the Taconic makes for a nice backdoor entry into New England and an even more scenic trip than the more heavily traveled New York State Thruway on the other side of the river. Most of the attractions described in this chapter, however, are clustered along the river itself and are mainly accessible via U.S. Route 9, once the carriage road that connected the feudal estates of Old Dutch New York. Franklin D. Roosevelt's Hyde Park and the sumptuous Vanderbilt estate are two of the valley's best-known latter-day country seats; in this chapter, though, we'll concentrate on less-publicized homesteads and other points of interest. The orientation is from south to north.

Just beyond the New York City limits, in Yonkers, **The Hudson River Museum** of Westchester occupies the magnificent 1876 Trevor Mansion and a cluster of recent additions designed to provide exhibition space. As the pre-eminent cultural institution of Westchester County and the lower Hudson Valley, the museum's resources reflect the natural, social, and artistic history of the area.

A visit to the Hudson River Museum includes a walk through the four meticulously restored rooms on the first floor of the mansion itself. You'll hardly find a better introduction to the short-lived but influential phase of Victorian taste known as the Eastlake style, marked by precise geometric carving and ornamentation—the traceries in the Persian carpets almost seem to be echoed in the furniture and ceiling details. Twenty years ago we might have found it all very fussy; now, it seems, we're not so sure.

Aside from the furnishings and personal objects that relate to the period when the Trevor family lived in the main building overlooking the Hudson, the museum's collections have grown to include impressive holdings of Hudson River School paintings, including work by Jasper Cropsey and Albert Bierstadt. The archives contain volumes on nineteenth- and twentieth-century history, art, and design, along with an architectural inventory of Westchester County. There's even a collection of representative Westchester mineral specimens.

In contrast to the period settings and historical emphases of the older parts of the museum, the state-of-the art Andrus Planetarium features the Zeiss M 1015 planetarium instrument, the only one of its kind in the Northeast. A contemporary orientation is also furthered by as many as thirty special art, science, and history exhibitions each year, many of them centered on the work of artists currently working in the Westchester area. There's an October-to-April series of chamber music concerts, and even a Victorian Christmas celebration.

The Hudson River Museum, Trevor Park-on-Hudson, 511 Warburton Avenue, Yonkers, NY 10701, (914) 963–4550, is open Wednesday, Friday, and Saturday, 10:00 A.M. to 5:00 P.M.; Sundays, noon to 5:00 P.M.; Thursdays, 10:00 A.M. to 9:00 P.M. Admission to the museum galleries is $2 for adults; $1 for senior citizens and children under 12. Admission to the planetarium is $3 for adults; $1 for senior citizens; and $1.50 for children under 12.

Hundreds of years before the Trevor Mansion was built, the Philipse family assembled a Westchester estate that makes the Trevors' 27 acres seem puny by comparison. Frederick Philipse the First came to what was then New Amsterdam in the 1650s and began using his sharp trader's instincts. By the 1690s, his lands encompassed the southern third of what is now Westchester County.

In 1716 Philipse's grandson, Frederick Philipse the Second, assumed the title of Lord of the Manor of Philipsborough. It was he who started construction of **Philipse Manor Hall,** now a state historic site housing a museum of eighteenth-century life among the Hudson Valley gentry. Following the inheritance of the estate in 1751 by Col. Frederick Philipse (the Third), the Georgian manor house was rebuilt and enlarged to become the family's year-round seat. Philipse planted elaborate gardens and imported the finest of furnishings for the Hall. His tenure as Lord of the Manor, however, ended when he decided to side with the Tory cause at the beginning of the American Revolution. He stayed for a while with his family in British-occupied New York City but evacuated to England along with His Majesty's troops at the end of the war.

Having been confiscated along with the rest of its Tory owner's properties after the Revolution, Philipse Manor Hall was auctioned by the state of New York and passed to a succession of private owners during the century that followed. The state purchased its former property in 1908 and has since maintained the mansion as a museum of the history, art, architecture, and upper-class life-style of pre-revolutionary New York. Inside and out, it remains one of the most perfectly preserved examples of Georgian style in the Northeast.

Philipse Manor Hall Historic Site, Warburton Avenue and Dock Street, Yonkers, NY 10702, (914) 965–4027, is open from noon to 5:00 P.M., Wednesday through Sunday; last tour at 4:30 P.M. These hours apply from late May through late October; call for winter schedule. Open also Memorial Day, Independence Day, and Labor Day; closed Thanksgiving, Christmas, and New Year's Day. Admission is free. Groups by reservation only.

The one-time owner of the house at our next stop would not have gotten along with Frederick Philipse III at all. He was Thomas Paine, arch-patriot, he who wrote of "the times that try men's souls." In 1784, one year after the formal end of the American Revolution which Paine had so vociferously fueled with his pamphlets, the state of New York granted him 300 acres, the site of what is now called the **Thomas Paine Cottage and Museum,** in reward for his services to the newly founded nation. Paine built the house in 1793. It originally stood atop the hill overlooking the later Paine Avenue but was relocated to the present site after being donated by its last private owner to the New Rochelle Huguenot Association in 1908. The Huguenot connection is not with Paine but with the town of New Rochelle, where the house stands. New Rochelle was founded by refugee members of the French Protestant sect in the late seventeenth century.

Although the author of "Common Sense" lived in this little house until his death in 1809, he didn't leave behind enough possessions to enable modern curators to maintain it entirely as a Paine memorial. Most of the actual Paine associations are concentrated in the rear room on the first floor, the "Paine Room." Here is a bullet hole beneath a window, made during an unsuccessful 1805 assassination attempt upon the writer; here also is one of the few authentic Franklin stoves, presented to Paine by Benjamin Franklin himself. There are also two chairs used by Paine when he boarded at a nearby tavern before his house was built.

The other rooms in the Paine Cottage contain artifacts relating to the colonial history of the New Rochelle area and its Huguenot settlers. Of particular interest is the Revolutionary period bed-room, with its exquisite handmade Star of Bethlehem quilt.

The Thomas Paine Cottage and Museum, 20 Sicard Avenue and (around the corner at) 983 North Avenue, New Rochelle, NY 10804, (914) 632–5376, is open from 2:00 P.M. to 5:00 P.M., Friday through Sunday in spring, summer, and fall, and by appointment the rest of the year. The suggested donation is $3 for adults; $1 for children under twelve.

Hop back onto Interstate 95, the New England Thruway, and head almost to the Connecticut border. Here, in Rye Brook, New York, you'll find the answer to the question that has nagged all of us since childhood: Where is the first house constructed entirely of reinforced concrete?

The answer is right here—Ward's Castle, built in 1876 by William E. Ward. But you needn't just stand outside to appreciate this crenellated and mansarded Victorian oddity, because it is open to the public as the **Museum of Cartoon Art.** Having fallen prey to whatever forces prey on concrete in its first hundred years, the Castle was placed on the National Register of Historic Places in 1976 and became the permanent home of the museum one year later. Renovations have since continued, with total restoration the ultimate goal.

The Museum of Cartoon Art was founded in 1974 by Mort Walker, creator of Beetle Bailey. It is dedicated to the acquisition, preservation, and exhibition of comic strips, comic books, maga-zine cartoons, editorial cartoons, animation art, and illustrative art. There are ongoing and special exhibits, film and video pro-grams, a lecture series, and a library open to researchers by ap-pointment. Patrons can even buy original cartoon art from the museum's gallery, as well as less expensive mementos from the gift shop.

The Museum of Cartoon Art, Comly Avenue, Rye Brook, NY 10573, (914) 939–0234, is open Tuesday through Friday, 10:00 A.M. to 4:00 P.M.; Sunday, 1:00 to 5:00 P.M. Admission is $3 for adults; $2 for senior citizens and students; $1 for children 5–12.

Reinforced concrete was nowhere in sight when the great Gothic Revival architect Alexander Jackson Davis designed **Lyndhurst** in 1838. Overlooking the broad expanse of the Tap-pan Zee from the east, this beautiful stone mansion and its land-scaped grounds are the property of the National Trust for Historic Preservation.

Lyndhurst, Tarrytown

Lyndhurst, built for former New York City Mayor William Paulding and originally called Paulding Manor or the Knoll, represented the full American flowering of the neo-Gothic aesthetic that had been sweeping England since the closing years of the eighteenth century. Davis and his fellow American Gothic architects and landscapists were striving for a quirkier, more romantic effect than that represented by the classical styles of the preceding century or the more recent Greek Revival, just as the Hudson River painters would soon show their disdain for the strictures of academic art.

Lyndhurst is unusual among American properties of its size and grandeur in having remained under private ownership for nearly a century and a quarter. Paulding and his son owned the estate until 1864, when it was purchased by a wealthy New York merchant named George Merritt. Merritt employed Davis to enlarge the house and to add its landmark tower; he also constructed a large greenhouse and several outbuildings. The greatest legacy of his stewardship, however, was the commencement of an ambitious program to develop an English-inspired romantic landscape to complement the Gothic architecture of the main house.

One of the most notorious of America's railroad robber barons, Jay Gould, acquired Lyndhurst in 1880. He maintained it as a country estate, spending the winter months in a Fifth Avenue mansion supplied with fresh flowers from an even larger Lyndhurst greenhouse of his own construction. Upon his death in 1892 Lyndhurst became the property of his older daughter Helen, who left it in turn to her younger sister Anna, Duchess of Talleyrand-Perigord, in 1938. The Duchess died in 1961, with instructions that the estate become the property of the National Trust.

Open to the public since 1964, Lyndhurst and its grounds are an impeccably maintained monument to the unbridled acquisitiveness of the Gilded Age, but more importantly, to the evolution of a certain style in American architecture, landscaping, and furniture design. The property is also the site of annual events such as a Rose Day, Sunset Serenades (a summer music series), dog show, and Christmas festivities, including candlelight tours on the first 3 weekends in December.

Lyndhurst, Route 9 just south of the Tappan Zee Bridge (635 S. Broadway) in Tarrytown, NY 10591, (914) 631–0046, is open May through October and also in December, Tuesday through Sunday, 10:00 A.M. to 5:00 P.M.; in November and from January through April, Saturday and Sunday, 10:00 A.M. to 5:00 P.M. Open on Monday holidays. Closed Thanksgiving, Christmas, and New Year's Day. Admission is $5 for adults; $4 for senior citizens; $3 for children 6–16.

Far less imposing than Lyndhurst but a good deal homier, **Sunnyside** stands just to the south, in Tarrytown, and offers a fascinating glimpse of the life of active retirement enjoyed there by its owner, Washington Irving. Irving described his country retreat as "a little old-fashioned stone mansion, all made up of gable ends, and as full of angles and corners as an old cocked hat." Not surprisingly for the man who wrote "The Legend of Sleepy Hollow," "Rip Van Winkle," and "Diedrich Knickerbocker's History of New York," Sunnyside is a step-gabled, Dutch Colonial affair, ivied with time and possessed of more than a little whimsy.

Washington Irving spent two periods of retirement at Sunnyside—the years 1836–42, and the last thirteen years of his

7

life, 1846–59. It was here that he wrote *Astoria,* his account of the Pacific Northwest, as well as *The Crayon Miscellany, Wolfert's Roost,* and *The Life of George Washington.* Here, also, the author entertained such visitors as Oliver Wendell Holmes, William Makepeace Thackeray, and Louis Napoleon. In the time not taken up with work and hospitality, he planned his own orchards, flower gardens, and arborways. These survive to this day, as do favorite Irving possessions such as the writing desk and piano on view in the house.

Sunnyside is owned and maintained by Historic Hudson Valley, which has also preserved four nearby attractions—Philipsburg Manor, in Upper Mills, a demonstration Dutch Colonial farm complete with working grist mill; Van Cortlandt Manor, in Croton-on-Hudson, once the baronial seat of the Van Cortlandt family; Montgomery Place, a large decorative estate at Annandale-on-Hudson, near Rhinebeck; and Union Church, Route 448 in Pocantico Hills, which includes stained-glass windows by Matisse and Chagall.

Sunnyside, West Sunnyside Lane (1 mile south of the Tappan Zee Bridge on Route 9), Tarrytown, NY 10591, (914) 631–8200 is open daily 10:00 A.M. to 5:00 P.M.; closed Thanksgiving, Christmas, and New Year's Day; and Tuesdays from December through March. Admission is $5 for adults; $4.50 for senior citizens; and $3 for children 6–14. The nearby attractions, other than Union Church, have similar hours and prices. Call Sunnyside for further information.

Another important figure of the early republic, political rather than literary, made his country home to the northeast at Katonah. This was John Jay, whom George Washington appointed to be first chief justice of the United States and who, with Alexander Hamilton and James Madison, was an author of the *Federalist Papers.* Jay retired to the farmhouse now known as the **John Jay Homestead** in 1801, after nearly three decades of public service, and lived here until his death in 1829.

John Jay was born in New York City in 1745. The son of a wealthy Huguenot merchant, he was educated at King's College (later Columbia University) and took up the practice of law just as the differences between Great Britain and her North American colonies were coming to a head. His political career began in 1774, when he was elected to the Continental Congress of which he was later president. He later served as minister to Spain, coauthor (with Benjamin Franklin and John Adams) of the Treaty of Paris ending the Revolution, Secretary for Foreign Affairs during the Articles of Confederation, and later, Supreme Court chief justice and negotiator of the Jay Treaty with Great Britain in 1794. Afterwards, he was elected to two terms as governor of New York under the provisions of the state constitution he had helped to write in 1777.

Finally, retired to his Westchester farmhouse, Jay busied himself with farming and horticulture, and with monitoring the early stirrings of the abolitionist movement, with which he was sympathetic. His son William and grandson John Jay II were also active abolitionists; inheriting the statesmanlike qualities of his grandfather, John Jay II also served as ambassador to Austria-Hungary. Both men lived at the old family homestead, as did John II's son, Col. William Jay II, a Civil War officer of the Union Army. The last Jay to live at the Katonah estate was Eleanor Jay Iselin, the Colonel's daughter. After her death in 1953, the property was offered for sale. It was purchased by Westchester County and turned over to the state of New York as a state historic site.

Having survived so long in the Jay family, the John Jay Homestead is still well stocked with furnishings and associated items that date back to the days when the great patriot lived here. Sixty acres of John Jay's original 900-acre farm are part of the State Historic Site which encompasses the homestead; the gardens and meadows make a lovely spot for a picnic or a quiet walk.

The John Jay Homestead State Historic Site, Route 22, Katonah, NY 10536, (914) 232–5651, is open May through December. Memorial Day to Labor Day, Wednesday through Saturday, 10:00 A.M. to 5:00 P.M.; Sunday, noon to 5:00 P.M. Call for off-season hours from September through December. The last tour enters the mansion at 4:00 P.M. Group tours are by advance reservation. Admission is free.

Not far from the Jay Homestead is another Katonah landmark, **Caramoor.** Perhaps the last of the truly grand private homes to have been built in the Hudson River Valley, Caramoor was constructed between 1929 and 1939 by Walter Tower Rosen, a Berlin-born lawyer and investment banker, as a country retreat and showplace for his growing collection of European paintings, sculpture, furnishings, and *objets d'art.* Rosen built his mansion in the Mediterranean style, incorporating into the building entire rooms removed from European châteaux and reassembled on the site.

Caramoor survives today not only as a house museum but as the home of an important summer music festival. Unlike many such programs, the Caramoor festival was not merely grafted onto a beautiful location but is a direct outgrowth of the interest and intentions of Walter Rosen and his wife, Lucie Bigelow Dodge Rosen. Both of the Rosens were accomplished amateur musicians, and they invited many well-known artists to Caramoor. A series of three concerts in the music room in 1946 was the genesis of today's Caramoor Music Festival, an institution nurtured by Mrs. Rosen during the years following her husband's death that year. In 1958 the addition of the Venetian Theater to the estate's complex of buildings made possible both larger audiences and more ambitious performances, including opera and ballet.

Two years after Mrs. Rosen's death in 1968, Caramoor was opened as a museum. The entire lower floor of the house is today open to the public, including the galleries containing the Rosens' collections of handpainted Chinese wallcoverings, fifth-century-B.C. Greek vases, English and Italian lacquer furniture, and Renaissance art. Each of the thirteen "period" rooms is a treasure in itself.

Caramoor, Girdle Ridge Road, Katonah, NY 10536, (914) 232–5035, is open from mid-May to mid-October on Thursdays and Saturdays, 11:00 A.M. to 4:00 P.M.; Sundays, 1:00 to 4:00 P.M. November through May, open Tuesday through Friday from 11:00 A.M. to 4:00 P.M. by appointment. Groups are welcome by appointment only. Admission is $4 for adults; $2 for children under 12. Caramoor Music Festival performances in the Venetian Theater and Spanish Courtyard take place throughout June, July, and August; for ticket information call the above number or write Caramoor, Box R, Katonah, NY 10536.

It takes an interesting region to supply the wherewithal for an interesting regional museum, and the town of Brewster in southern Putnam County has done a good job of filling the bill for the **Southeast Museum.** Brewster has been the center of a diverse number of enterprises, including mining, railroading, circuses, and even the manufacture of condensed milk. Reminders of all of these phases of local development are on exhibit at the museum, which is housed in the 1896 Town Hall of the community once known as Southeast.

Southeast was settled long before the Brewster family rose to prominence in the 1840s and 1850s, lending their name to the community that grew up around the railroad depot. The first settlers came about 1725. For more than one hundred years their main pursuits were agriculture and modest local trade. In the mid-nineteenth century, though, Brewster's economic horizons expanded through the arrival of the Harlem Railroad, later part of Commodore Vanderbilt's vast New York Central System. Railroad days in Brewster are represented at the museum by the artifacts in the David McLane collection.

There was plenty for the Harlem Line to carry. Around the time of the Civil War, the local Tilly Foster mine was an important source of various ores and minerals; a mineralogical collection related to the mine's output is on display at the museum. Another Civil War–era pursuit that became a cornerstone of the local economy was the condensed milk industry, which began when area resident Gail Borden—at President Lincoln's urging—developed a process to evaporate the water from milk and preserve it for use by troops in the field. The Borden exhibit at the Southeast Museum chronicles the fifty-year history of the company's presence in Brewster, which came to an end when dairy farming declined in the area.

Brewster was also winter quarters for a number of circuses in the past century, and more than a few of the town's residents found employment in the traveling troupes. Many of these small local enterprises were later consolidated by P. T. Barnum, who hailed from just across the state line in Connecticut. This most colorful aspect of Brewster's past is recalled in the museum's collection of early American circus memorabilia.

Finally, vestiges of the prosperity brought about by all this activity survive in the Southeast's Victorian collection, which preserves a cross section of the furnishings and personal effects of a comfortable household of the era.

The Southeast Museum, Main Street, Brewster, NY 10509, (914) 279-7500, is open Tuesday through Thursday from noon to 4:00 P.M.; Saturdays and Sundays from 2:00 P.M. to 4:00 P.M. Admission is free.

There was something about the Hudson River Valley that brought out the feudal lord in people with the means to do something about it—a natural invitation, as it were, to create surroundings commensurate with the stately grandeur of the river itself. The wealthy landowner States Morris Dyckman answered the call in 1804. He built a country seat, called **Boscobel,** that was and is one of the glories of Federal architecture in the United States.

Boscobel was also one of the great triumphs of historic preservation in an era, the 1950s, notorious for its disregard and wanton destruction of fine old buildings. Threatened with being leveled to make way for new construction, Boscobel was rescued largely through the generosity of *Reader's Digest* cofounder Lila Acheson Wallace. The building was dismantled and reassembled, piece by piece, on its present site in Garrison-on-Hudson, 15 miles north of its old foundations.

Boscobel today looks inside and out much as it did in Dyckman's day, although the shade of the old patrician might well wonder how his house managed to move. The Federal-period furnishings include work by New York's own Duncan Phyfe, and much of Dyckman's own collections of porcelain, silver, and finely bound books have been returned. Outside, formal rose gardens and an apple orchard suggest the landscaping of a country estate of the early nineteenth century.

Boscobel Restoration, Inc., the nonprofit organization that maintains the house, also schedules a program of special seasonal events to which Dyckman's relocated mansion makes a perfect backdrop. These include spring garden parties, nature walks, a summer concert series, and Christmas candlelight tours. Christmas, by the way, is an especially good time to visit Boscobel's gift shop.

Boscobel, Route 9D, Garrison-on-Hudson, NY 10524, (914) 265–3638, is open daily except Tuesdays and the months of January and February; it's also closed on Thanksgiving and Christmas. April through October, the hours are 9:30 A.M. to 5:00 P.M. (last tour at 4:15); November, December, and March hours are 9:30 A.M. to 4:00 P.M., with the last tour at 3:15. Admission is $5 for adults; $4 for senior citizens; $2.50 for children 6–14.

Not all of the Hudson Valley landowners were as well-to-do as States Dyckman; most, of course, were burghers of a far more modest stamp. The legacy of the life led by one such family is preserved in the **Van Wyck Homestead,** east of the river in Fishkill. The house was begun in 1732 by Cornelius Van Wyck, who had purchased his nearly 1,000 acres of land from an earlier 85,000-acre Dutchess County estate, and completed in the 1750s with the construction of the West Wing. For all the land its owners possessed, the homestead is nevertheless a modest affair, a typical Dutch country farmhouse.

Like so many other farmhouses, the Van Wyck Homestead might have been forgotten by history had it not played a part in the Revolutionary War. Located as it was along the strategic route between New York City and the Champlain Valley, the house was requisitioned by the Continental Army to serve as headquarters for Gen. Israel Putnam. Fishkill served as an important supply

Boscobel, Garrison-on-Hudson

depot for Gen. Washington's northern forces from 1776 to 1783. Military trials were held at the house; one such event was reputedly the source used by James Fenimore Cooper for an incident in his novel *The Spy*.

Another factor leading to the homestead's preservation was its having reverted back to the Van Wyck Family after the Revolution ended. Descendants of its builder lived here for more than 150 years. Today it is operated by the Fishkill Historical Society as a museum of colonial life in the Hudson Valley, containing period furniture and everyday household paraphernalia. An interesting sidelight is the exhibit of Revolutionary War artifacts unearthed in the vicinity during archaeological "digs" sponsored by the Society.

The Van Wyck Homestead, Snook Road (near the intersection of Routes 9 and 84), Fishkill, NY 12524, (914) 896–9560, is open by appointment only. Bus tours are welcome.

Heading north past Poughkeepsie, we're back in mansion territory—but with a difference. Homes such as Philipse Manor Hall and Boscobel were built by men whose fortunes were founded in vast landholdings, but palaces such as the **Mills Mansion** in Staatsburg represent the glory days of industrial and financial captains—the so-called Gilded Age of the late nineteenth century. The idea behind this sort of house building was not to live like a country squire but like a Renaissance doge.

Ogden Mills's neoclassical mansion was finished in 1896, but its story begins more than a hundred years before. In 1792 the property on which it stands was purchased by Morgan Lewis, great-grandfather of Mills's wife Ruth Livingston Mills. Lewis, an officer in the Revolution and third post-independence governor of New York State, built two houses here. The first burned in 1832, at which time it was replaced by an up-to-date Greek Revival structure. This was the home that stood on the property when it was inherited by Ruth Livingston Mills in 1888.

Greek revival was all very nice, but Ogden Mills had something far grander in mind for his wife's legacy. He hired a firm with a solid reputation in mansion building to enlarge the home and embellish its interiors—a popular firm among wealthy clients, that went by the name of McKim, Mead, and White.

The architects added two spacious wings and decked out both the new and old portions of the exterior with balustrades and pilasters more reminiscent of Blenheim Palace than anything previously seen in the Hudson Valley. The interior was (and is) French, in Louis XV and XVI period styles—lots of carving and gilding on furniture and wall and ceiling surfaces, along with oak paneling and monumental tapestries. The artwork displayed within the house includes several portraits of members of New York's prominent Livingston family, to which Mrs. Mills was related.

The Mills family spent autumns at Staatsburg, dividing the rest of the year among four other homes in the United States and abroad. The last of the clan to live here was Ogden L. Mills, at one time U.S. Secretary of the Treasury, who died in 1937. At that time one of his surviving sisters donated the home to the state of New York, which opened it to the public as a state historic site.

The Mills Mansion, off Old Post Road, Staatsburg, NY 12580, (914) 889–4100, is open from early May through Labor Day, Wednesday through Saturday, 10:00 A.M. to 5:00 P.M.; Sunday, 1:00 to 5:00 P.M. From Labor Day through the last Sunday in October, the mansion is open Wednesday through Saturday from noon to 5:00 P.M.; Sunday, 1:00 to 5:00 P.M. The mansion is also open during the Christmas season. Call for hours. Admission is free.

No more mansions for a while. Continuing north along the Hudson, the next point of interest is the **Old Rhinebeck Aerodrome,** 3 miles upriver from the town of Rhinebeck. Proprietor and curator Cole Palen has made the Aerodrome more than just a museum—many of the pre-1930s planes exhibited here actually take to the air each weekend.

The three main buildings at the Aerodrome house a collection of aircraft, automobiles, and other vehicles from the period 1900–1937 and are open throughout the week. On Saturdays and Sundays, though, you can combine a tour of the exhibits on the ground with attendance at an air show featuring both original aircraft and accurate reproductions. Saturday is reserved for flights of planes from the Pioneer (pre-World War I) and Lindbergh eras. On Sunday, the show is a period-piece melodrama in which intrepid Allied fliers do battle with the "Black Baron." Where else can you watch a live dogfight?

All that's left at this point is to go up there yourself, and you can do just that. The Aerodrome has on hand a 1929 New Standard D-25, which carries four passengers wearing helmets and goggles—for open-cockpit flights of fifteen-minutes duration. The cost is $20 per person.

Old Rhinebeck Aerodrome, Taconic Parkway Exit 199, Rhinebeck, NY 12572, (914) 758–8610, is open daily, May 15 through the end of October, from 10:00 A.M. to 5:00 P.M. The air shows, from June 15 through October 15, take place on Saturdays and Sundays at 2:30 and 4:00 P.M. Biplane rides are available before and after the shows. Weekday admission is $3 for adults; $1 for children 6–10. Saturday and Sunday air-show admission is $8 for adults; $4 for children. The plane rides cost extra, as mentioned above.

Crailo Gardens, in the small town of Ancram, near the spot where the borders of New York, Massachusetts, and Connecticut meet, is a place to contemplate earthbound delights rather than aerial excitement. The Crailo Gardens and Nurseries represent more than a quarter century of devotion on the part of founder Edwin R. Thomson to the cultivation of dwarf and rare conifers. Thomson's collection now exceeds 400 cultivars of *Chamaecyparis, Juniperus, Picea, Pinus, Thuja,* and others; he has some 3,000 plants for sale and starts about 1,000 each year. All of the plants that are available for sale are in containers, with the exception of those in a permanent exhibit area, which is open to the public after 2:00 P.M. on Sunday afternoons from May through September. At other times of the year, an appointment is advised.

Why focus upon dwarf evergreens? "Dwarfs are becoming more popular," Mr. Thomson responds, "because they do not grow out of scale so rapidly as standard landscape plants do." As for the business of collecting and selling the diminutive trees and shrubs, the gardener is even more succinct: "I have some very beautiful plants which I enjoy greatly."

Crailo Gardens, Route 82, Ancram, NY 12502, (518) 329–0601, is open to visitors during the above-mentioned summer hours. Admission is free.

There was a time when every schoolchild worthy of a gold star on his or her reports knew the name *Clermont.* Of course—it was the first successful steamboat, built by Robert Fulton and tested on the Hudson River. Less commonly known, however, is that the boat, formally registered by its owners as *The North River Steamboat of Clermont,* took its name from the estate of Robert Livingston, chancellor of New York and a backer of Fulton's experiments. **Clermont,** one of the great family seats of the valley, overlooks the Hudson River in Germantown.

The story of Clermont begins with the royal charter granted to Robert Livingston in 1686, which made the Scottish-born trader Lord of the Manor of Livingston, a 162,000-acre tract that would evolve into the entire southern third of modern-day Columbia County. When Livingston died in 1728, he broke with the English custom of strict adherence to primogeniture, giving 13,000 acres of his land to his third son. This was Clermont, the Lower Manor, on which Robert of Clermont, as he was known, built his home in 1730.

Two more Robert Livingstons figure in the tale after this point. The first, Robert of Clermont's son, was a New York judge who early championed the colonial cause against Great Britain. The second was the judge's son, Robert R. Livingston, a member of the Second Continental Congress who later filled the now-obsolete office of state chancellor. It was the chancellor's mother, Margaret Beekman Livingston, who rebuilt the house after it was burned in 1777 by the British (parts of the original walls are incorporated into the present structure), and the chancellor himself who, after the war, began to indulge the scientific curiosity that led to his partnership with Robert Fulton. The *Clermont*, which its builders always called the *North River* or simply the *Steam-boat*, stopped at the estate's dock during its 1807 maiden voyage. After a winter of major modifications, the boat that we now refer to by the name of her home port went into regular service.

The Livingston family lived at Clermont until 1962, making various enlargements and modifications to their home over time. In 1962 the house, its furnishings, and the 500 remaining acres of the Clermont estate became the property of the state of New York.

Clermont State Historic Site (also a National Historic Landmark) makes a fine place for an indoor or outdoor visit. The mansion itself has been restored to its circa 1930 appearance; however, the collections are primarily half eighteenth- and half nineteenth-century French and Early American. Tours of Clermont include the first and second floors. The newly restored carriage barn houses a Visitors' Center that offers a gift shop, an orientation exhibit, and a short film. The historic grounds offer walks through formal gardens, woodsy hiking trails, and spacious landscapes (perfect for picnics) on bluffs overlooking the Hudson.

Clermont, off Route 9G, Clermont, NY 12526, (518) 537–4240, is open from May 1 through Labor Day weekend, Wednesday through Saturday, 10:00 A.M. to 5:00 P.M.; Sunday, 1:00 to 5:00 P.M.; also 10:00 A.M. to 5:00 P.M. on Memorial Day, Independence Day, and Labor Day. From the Tuesday after Labor Day through October 31, the hours are noon to 5:00 P.M. Wednesday through Saturday; 1:00 to 5:00 P.M. Sunday. These hours apply to tours of the Livingston home; the grounds are open daily year-round, 8:30 A.M. to sunset. Admission is free.

History generally conditions us to expect the great houses of the world to belong to industrialists and landholders, while artists—so the cliché has it—starve in garrets. One artist who

Olana, Hudson

built many fanciful garrets and starved in none of them was the Hudson River School master Frederic Edwin Church, whose Persian Gothic castle **Olana** commands a magnificent view of the river in the town of Hudson. What the popular landscape painter did here was nothing less than sculpt the perfect embodiment of his tastes and then live in it for the rest of his life.

Church had been a commercial and critical success for more than a decade when he decided to build his castle on the Hudson property he and his wife had purchased in 1860. In 1867 and 1868 the Churches had traveled throughout Europe and the Middle East, and the trip made quite an impression on their sensibilities as reflected in the thirty-seven-room mansion they began building in 1870. Olana, which was completed four years later, draws heavily upon Islamic and Byzantine motifs. Persian arches abound, as do Oriental carpets, brasswork, and inlaid furniture. The overall setting is typically Victorian, with no space left empty that could possibly be filled with things. What makes Olana untypical, of course, is the quality of the things.

18

Although Church employed as a consultant Calvert Vaux, who had collaborated with Frederick Law Olmsted on the design of New York's Central Park, the artist was the architect of his own house. When scholars describe Olana as a major work of art by Church, they are not speaking figuratively; the paints for the interior were mixed on his own palette.

Church also designed Olana's landscaping as a three-dimensional work of art, and the views afforded by the site—500 feet above the Hudson—are skillfully exploited on every side.

Church's youngest son inherited Olana in 1900, and the artist's daughter-in-law lived here until her death in 1964. Fortunately, an ad hoc organization called Olana Preservation Inc. acted to protect the house and secure its purchase by the state of New York, which in 1966 placed Olana on its register of historic sites.

Olana, Route 9G, Hudson, NY 12534, (518) 828–0135, is open *by guided tour only* from May 1 to Labor Day, Wednesday through Sunday. The first tour begins at 10:00 A.M. weekdays and Saturdays and 12:00 P.M. on Sundays; the last tour starts at 4:00 P.M. Also open on Memorial Day, Independence Day, and Labor Day. Telephone regarding September and October hours. As Olana tours are limited to twelve people at a time (tours last approximately forty-five minutes), the site's managers recommend that visitors call ahead for tour reservations. Space will be held until fifteen minutes before tour time. An admission fee is charged. The grounds are open year-round from 8:00 A.M. until sunset.

As fascinating as Olana is, by the time you leave you may be humming the old Shaker tune "It's a Gift to Be Simple." So, head north and east to the **Shaker Museum** in Old Chatham. The museum is housed in a collection of buildings located just 12 miles from Mt. Lebanon, New York, where the Shakers established the community that was to become their motherhouse in 1787.

The Shakers, formally known as the United Society of Believers in Christ's Second Appearing, was a sect founded in Britain and transplanted to America just prior to the Revolution. A quietist, monastic order dedicated to equality between the sexes, sharing of community property, temperance in its broad sense, and the practice of celibacy, the sect peaked in the mid-nineteenth century with about six thousand members. Today, there are fewer than ten Shakers living in two New England communities.

Ironically, it is the secular aspects of Shaker life that are most often recalled today. The members of the communities were almost obsessive regarding simplicity and purity of form in the articles that they designed and crafted for daily life; "Shaker furniture" has become a generic term for the elegantly uncluttered designs they employed. In their pursuit of the perfect form dictated by function, they even invented now-ubiquitous objects such as the clothespin and the flat broom.

The Shaker Museum has amassed a collection of more than seventeen thousand objects, half of which are on display. The main building contains an orientation gallery that surveys Shaker history and provides highlights of the rest of the collection; a furniture gallery; a kitchen setting; a medicine shop; a laundry-room setting; and blacksmithing and coopering tools. The main building's newest exhibit, entitled *A Room of Shaker Furniture: Forty Untouched Masterpieces of American Design,* showcases the Museum's finest pieces of Shaker furniture. Previously in storage, these pieces have never been in the hands of collectors and have never been altered by any outside source. The Craft Building contains a new gallery, Shaker cabinetmakers' tools and machines; an exhibition of Shaker life in the twentieth century; a display of more than 300 baskets; and a broom-making display. Another building is set up as a schoolroom, and there is a small herb garden used for specimen purposes only. The museum's library contains one of the two most extensive collections of Shaker material in the world. A store on the grounds even sells reproductions of the sect's famous furniture and tidy oval boxes. The Museum Cafe serves light lunches and beverages.

The Shaker Museum, Shaker Museum Road (off County Route 13), Old Chatham, NY 12136, (518) 794–9100, is open daily, May 1 through October 31, from 10:00 A.M. to 5:00 P.M. There are evening hours during the summer months. Admission is $5.50 for adults; $4 for senior citizens; $3 for children ages 8–17; and free for children age 8 or under. Family admission is $12.

When we think of the Dutch in America, we generally recall only the settlement of New Amsterdam, later New York, at the mouth of the Hudson River. But the colony of "New Netherland" actually extended as far north along the valley as Albany—or rather, Fort Orange, which is what the Dutch called their northern outpost in the seventeenth century. Just across the river from Albany, in Rensselaer, stands **Crailo,** an early house that recalls a time when the Dutch were still the predominant cultural presence in this area, despite their loss of political control to the British.

When Crailo was the center of preparations for the French and Indian Wars, the Dutch had already been in the vicinity of Albany for more than a century. Present-day Rensselaer and environs were colonized in the 1630s; the town name itself was that of the family who held the "patroonship," virtually a feudal proprietorship, of this vast area on the east bank of the Hudson. Crailo itself was occupied by Hendrick Van Rensselaer, heir to a substantial portion of the estate.

Crailo changed with time and tastes. It received the Georgian treatment, complete with a new east wing, in 1762; at the beginning of the 1800s, another Van Rensselaer added Federal touches. The house passed out of family hands and suffered through a variety of uses, only to be purchased by descendant Susan DeLancey Van Rensselaer Strong in 1899 and donated to the state twenty-five years later. (The late Ms. Strong's name, by the way, is about as aristocratic as you can get in New York circles—sort of an Empire State equivalent of Cabot Lodge in New England.) Since 1933 the house has been maintained as a museum.

Appropriately, the state parks authorities decided that the focus of the exhibits at Crailo would be the story of the early Dutch settlements in the upper Hudson Valley. The house has been fitted up as a museum of the Dutch roots of Albany and the Valley. Displays include artifacts from Fort Orange, furs, paintings, Dutch furniture, and household objects unique to the Hudson Valley. On special occasions, visitors can even watch demonstrations of eighteenth-century cooking. There are also outdoor concerts and an annual Twelfth Night celebration. The museum has extensive school programs, including a cooking class, by appointment.

Crailo, 9½ Riverside Avenue, Rensselaer, NY 12144, (518) 463–8738, is open April through December 15, Wednesday through Saturday, 10:00 A.M. to 5:00 P.M., 1:00 to 5:00 P.M. on Sunday. Also open Memorial Day, Independence Day, and Labor Day. Telephone for off-season hours. Admission is free.

Natural as well as social history are the focus of a Troy institution geared specifically to young people. This is the **Rensselaer County Junior Museum,** a "hands-on" learning center that has everything from a reproduction of a circa-1850 log cabin to constellation shows in a "Sky Dome" theater.

The main gallery of the museum features annually changing art, history, and science exhibits. Upstairs, in addition to the cabin and its furnishings, there is a gallery of physical- and natural-science exhibits which includes honeybees in an observation hive, a red-tailed hawk, live reptiles, and both salt- and fresh-water aquariums. Downstairs, the major exhibit is a large-scale diorama depicting life in a beaver pond.

If you live in the Troy area, look into the Junior Museum's schedule of kids' trips to area zoos, wildlife sanctuaries, whale watches, and other museums. There's even a performing arts series.

The Rensselaer County Junior Museum, 282 Fifth Avenue, Troy, NY 12182, (518) 235–2120, is open Saturday through Wednesday, from 1:00 to 5:00 P.M. The other days of the week are reserved for group tours, except during spring and winter school vacations, when public visiting hours are extended. Admission is by a suggested donation of $1.50 per person and includes shows in both the Sky Dome theater and in the conference room, with live animals.

Most of us have heard by now that the Battle of Bunker Hill was not actually fought on Bunker Hill (it took place on Breed's Hill, also in Charlestown, Massachusetts), but how many can identify another military misnomer of the Revolution?

Don't all raise your hands at once. We're talking about the 1777 Battle of Bennington, an American victory that laid the groundwork for the defeat and surrender of General Burgoyne at Saratoga that October. The battle, in which American militiamen defended their ammunition and supplies from an attacking party made up of British troops, Tory sympathizers, mercenaries, and Indians, took place not in Bennington, Vermont, but in Walloomsac, New York. True, the stores that the British were after were stashed in the Vermont town, but the actual fighting took place on New York soil. This is a detail that may rattle some Vermonters, who not only possess a Bennington Battle Monument but also a lingering resentment of the "Yorkers" who once threatened to annex their mountain fastness. But that's another story.

The state of New York today maintains the site of the battle as an official state historic site. It's on a lovely hilltop in eastern Rensselaer County, studded with bronze and granite markers that explain the movements of the troops on the American militia's triumphal day. The spot is located on the north side of Route 67 and is open throughout the year during daylight hours, weather permitting. Visitors can check road conditions by calling **Bennington Battlefield,** (518) 686–7109. On a clear day, visitors can enjoy fine views of the Green Mountain foothills, prominent among which is Bennington's obelisk monument. Drive over to visit the monument and give the Vermonters their due—but really, doesn't "Battle of Walloomsac" have a nice ring to it?

The last stop on this ramble up the east shore of the Hudson offers proof that the monastic spirit did not pass into history in this part of the world with the Shakers. Cambridge, New York, is the home of the **New Skete Communities,** a group of monks, nuns, and lay people organized around a life of prayer, contemplation, and physical work. Founded in 1966 within the Byzantine Rite of the Roman Catholic Church, the New Skete Communities have since 1979 been a part of the Orthodox Church in America.

Skete is a term that applies to small monastic communities with a single spiritual leader, as opposed to the larger monasteries or convents affiliated with worldwide religious orders. The original Skete was an Egyptian community of the fourth century, where early Christians went to pray and live apart from the world. The leader of the Cambridge group is Father Laurence, under whose guidance the monks first organized two decades ago. The New Skete Communities have since 1966 included the Nuns of New Skete, whose monastery is 5 miles from here, and more recently grew to incorporate the Companions of New Skete, a group of three married couples and one widow who live according to a religious rule of life in a separate house at the monastery proper.

Visitors to new Skete are welcome at two of the community's houses of worship. The small Church of the Transfiguration of Christ, open at all times, contains a number of icons painted by the monks, while the larger Church of Christ the Wisdom of God—open to visitors only during services—has original pieces of mosaic, imbedded in its marble floor, which were brought from the A.D. 576 Church of Sancta Sophia (Holy Wisdom) in Constantinople. Constantinople, of course, is now Istanbul, and Sancta Sophia is a museum.

As with many monastic communities, the monks and the nuns of New Skete help support themselves through secular pursuits. At New Skete, their business is the breeding of German shepherds and the boarding and training of all breeds. The monks have even written a successful book, *How to Be Your Dog's Best Friend.* They also operate a gift shop at the monastery, where they sell their own cheeses, smoked meats, fruitcake, and the famous New Skete cheesecakes.

For information regarding visiting times, the schedule of religious service, and the sale of *New Skete Farms* products, call the New Skete Communities at (518) 677-3928. The monastery is located on New Skete Road, accessible from Cambridge center via East Main Street and Chestnut Hill Road.

Off the Beaten Path in the Adirondacks

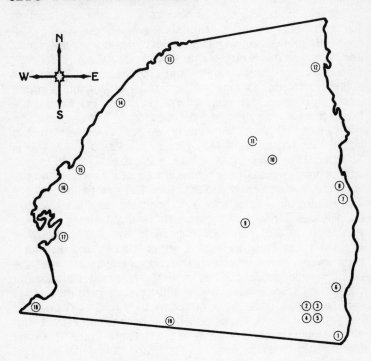

1. Saratoga National Historical Park
2. Saratoga Spa State Park
3. National Museum of Racing and Hall of Fame
4. The Casino
5. Petrified Gardens
6. Hyde Collection
7. Fort Ticonderoga
8. Crown Point State Historic Site
9. Adirondack Museum
10. John Brown Farm State Historic Site
11. Six Nations Indian Museum
12. Kent-Delord House
13. St. Lawrence Seaway
14. Frederic Remington Art Museum
15. Boldt Castle
16. Thousand Islands Shipyard Museum
17. Sackets Harbor Battlefield
18. Fort Ontario
19. Steuben Memorial

The Adirondacks

North of the Mohawk Valley, spread between Lake Champlain and the Saint Lawrence River, New York's Adirondack Mountains comprise one of the nation's great expanses of near-wilderness and surely the largest slice of backcountry in the Northeastern states. The state-protected Adirondack Forest Preserve alone accounts for more than two million acres of mountains, woodlands, and lakes, and this is only part of the six-million-acre Adirondack State Park. For sheer vastness and emptiness, the Adirondack region is rivaled in this part of the country only by the northern interior of Maine; but while inland Maine—except for the Katahdin massif—is generally flat or gently rolling, the northern counties of New York contain forty-two peaks over 4,000 feet in height. (The highest is Mt. Marcy, near Lake Placid, at 5,344 feet.) As in northern Maine, parts of the Adirondacks are still logged, although many areas have returned to a near-approximation of what they looked like when white men first saw them.

Ironically, the Adirondacks have benefited from being left on the sidelines during the "discovery" of nearby Vermont and New Hampshire in the years following World War II. The two New England states have acquired a certain cachet, and they have been more heavily developed and populated as a result. The equally beautiful Adirondacks, meanwhile, have drifted along in the public consciousness largely as the place where the famous summer chairs come from (it seems they really did originate here) and as the locale for Gilded-Age "camps" on estates running into the tens of thousands of acres. Throw in the Thousand Islands, Saranac Lake, and lakes Placid and George, and the perception is complete.

But there's so much more. In addition to being a "hidden" wilderness recreation land of such vast proportions, the Adirondacks have numerous historical connections, particularly in the form of battlefields that saw clashes between British and American forces when the region was a frontier buffer between Canada and the new republic to the south. Today's border is marked by the engineering marvel of the Saint Lawrence Seaway, and by the binational resort area that has sprung up around the Thousand Islands. The southeastern gateway to the Adirondacks, Saratoga, is one of the horse-racing capitals of America. Farther north are museums that chronicle the life of the Iroquois, the art of Frederic Remington, and Adirondacks craftsmanship, boat building, and pioneer life.

Head north beyond Saratoga, then, for the real "upstate" New York, a domain that rivals the expansiveness of the West yet is rooted in the traditions of the East.

(Note: the overall place-to-place direction followed in this chapter is counterclockwise—north, then west and south.)

North of the confluence of the Mohawk and Hudson rivers, near the present-day towns of Mechanicville and Stillwater, one of the most decisive battles of world history was fought in the early days of October, 1777. Neither a great slaughter like Verdun nor a final checkmate like Waterloo, the Battle of Saratoga holds its place in history as a watershed, a turning point in the prolonged and peripatetic series of military campaigns that made up the American Revolution. The battle, the sites of which are commemorated in **Saratoga National Historical Park,** offered the first conclusive proof that American forces could triumph over the British in a major engagement and led to the French entering the war on behalf of the United States.

The Lake Champlain and Hudson River valleys were a major north-south route in the eighteenth century and consequently provided a natural highway for the movement of troops. British Gen. John Burgoyne planned, early in 1777, to move his forces southward from Canada to Albany, from which point he would be able to act in concert with the British army headquartered in New York to cut the New England colonies off from the Middle Atlantic region. But Burgoyne's plan ran into trouble from the start. He was denied the support of a detachment under Col. Barry St. Leger proceeding east from Lake Ontario, after St. Leger retreated back to Canada in the face of an expected attack by Gen. Benedict Arnold (Arnold was not yet the traitor of historical record). Burgoyne also suffered a surprise defeat when he sent part of his army into the field against New England militia at the Battle of Bennington. By the time he reached the west bank of the Hudson at Saratoga (present-day Schuylerville) on September 13, the prospect of "Gentleman Johnny" Burgoyne making an easy progress to Albany was considerably dimmed by the presence of 9,000 American troops, with artillery, guarding the Hudson River route at Bemis Heights.

Burgoyne was stopped in a standoff battle on September 19. He regrouped his forces a mile north of the American lines for a three-week period of waiting for reinforcements from New York. But help didn't arrive, and rather than allow his supplies to become even more depleted and his men more demoralized, Burgoyne again

The Saratoga Monument

engaged the Americans in battle on October 7. The fighting ended with a thousand British casualties (the Americans suffered fewer than half that number) and a Redcoat retreat north to the Saratoga heights. It was there that Burgoyne, his 6,000 troops surrounded by 20,000 Americans, surrendered on October 17.

Saratoga National Historical Park encompasses all of the sites crucial to the engagements of those fateful weeks in September and October of 1777. Starting at the park's Visitor Center, a 9-mile tour road connects ten stops at which explanations of the battle are offered. The 1777 Philip Schuyler House contains late-eighteenth-century furnishings and remains in a detached area of the park; Neilson House is the only building that remained on the battlefield. Both homes can be toured. Also on the park grounds is the Saratoga Monument, a 155-foot embellished obelisk dedicated in 1912. The 2,600 acres of the park are accessible for nonmotorized outdoor recreation such as bicycling, cross-country skiing, horseback riding, and hiking.

Saratoga National Historical Park Visitor Center, Route 32, Stillwater, NY 12170, (518) 664–9821, is open daily in July and August, from 9:00 A.M. to 6:00 P.M. Historic Schuyler House and Neilson House are open Memorial Day through Labor Day; Tuesday through Sunday, 9:00 A.M. to 5:00 P.M. Ranger tours; no charge. Admission is $3 per car for the tour road; $1 for hiking; children 16 and under, free.

Saratoga Spa State Park is only a few miles to the north and west, but it celebrates nothing so serious as battles and surrenders. The emphasis here is on water, in particular the famous "waters" that made Saratoga an elegant resort in the 1880s and still lure both the convinced and merely curious to investigate their supposed restorative powers.

Twenty-two separate mineral wells currently bubble up from the ground in and around Saratoga State Park. All of their waters are naturally carbonated, although they are significantly different in taste, alkalinity, and salinity, and the effects they produce (some are decidedly laxative). The springs that release these waters from their deep artesian wells were first discovered by the Indians, but it was nineteenth-century entrepreneurs and vacationers who built up their reputation as curatives. A hundred years ago, the springs were tapped and the waters served at salons built for the purpose; "taking the waters" became as much a part of summering at Saratoga as frequenting the racetrack.

In 1910 New York State acquired the rights to the mineral waters of Saratoga—a measure that was required to prevent the eventual depletion of the supply—and began to purchase the land that would become the State Park. Although the springs still flow and some of the waters are bottled (some are available for drinking on site), the principal means of enjoyment for latter-day enthusiasts is in the famous Saratoga baths. There are two state-run bathhouses at Saratoga, the Lincoln (open only during July and August) and the Roosevelt, named after President Franklin Roosevelt, who sought relief from his polio affliction at Saratoga. Open all year, the Roosevelt Baths offer private rooms, reasonable rates for mineral baths and soothing massages, and even hydrocollator and hot-pack treatments. For the baths, the effervescent water is heated to exactly body temperature, and the resulting effect is one of not quite knowing where your body leaves off and the water begins. It's hard to imagine anything more relaxing.

There's a lot more to Saratoga Spa State Park than the waters. Under contract with the state, a private firm operates the comfortable Gideon Putnam Hotel, set right on the park grounds within a short walk of the baths as well as a fine golf course, tennis courts, and cross-country ski trails. There are two swimming pools, one Olympic-sized, and in the winter, three ice skating rinks. The Saratoga Performing Arts Center is the summer home of both the Philadelphia Orchestra and the New York City Ballet, as well as the venue for a full schedule of pop concerts and dramatic performances in the Little Theater. Nearby, the town of Saratoga Springs offers lodging, dining, and of course the celebrated racetrack.

Saratoga Spa State Park, Saratoga Springs, NY 12866, (518) 584-2535, is open throughout the year. For information on the baths and related treatments, call (518) 584-2011. For ticket information for the Saratoga Performing Arts Center, call (518) 587-3330.

After a nice mineral bath and massage you'll be all set for a night at the track. Horse racing is Saratoga's other *raison d'etre,* and the history and traditions of the sport are thoroughly chronicled at the **National Museum of Racing and Hall of Fame,** Saratoga Springs. Located directly across from Saratoga Race Course, the nation's oldest thoroughbred track, the museum recently completed a six-million-dollar renovation. Patrons enter the museum through an actual starting gate, complete with life-size representations of a horse, jockey, and starter. Some of the highlights: 300 oil paintings of outstanding horses and a collection of 200 sets of colorful racing silks; the saddle and boots used by jockey Johnny Loftus on Man O' War; a Hall of Fame for famous horses, jockeys, and trainers; an actual skeleton of a thoroughbred; and bronze equine sculptures. An eighteen-minute feature film, *Race America,* was filmed at racetracks and stud farms across the country and is shown in the newly renovated, state-of-the-art theater. Video booths lining the walls provide films of some of racing's greatest moments. There is a gift shop.

The National Museum of Racing and Hall of Fame, Union Avenue, Saratoga Springs, NY 12866, (518) 584–0400, is open year-round. From Labor Day to Memorial Day, open Tuesday through Saturday, 10:00 A.M. to 4:30 P.M. From Memorial Day through August 1, open Monday through Saturday, 10:00 A.M. to 4:30 P.M., and Sunday, noon to 4:00 P.M. During racing season, August 2–28, open daily, 9:30 A.M. to 6:00 P.M. Admission is $2 for adults; $1 for senior citizens, students, and children 5–18.

Before leaving Saratoga, stop in at **The Casino,** which actually was one back in the days when it was perfectly legal to lose your shirt at the blackjack tables in New York State. The handsome Victorian structure was built 1870–71 by John Morrissey, a colorful local character who was equally at home in the boxing ring and the state senate and who was one of the founders of the first racetrack at Saratoga Springs in 1863. Morrissey and the next owner, Richard Canfield, both ran a lucrative gambling establishment here, especially after Canfield's 1894 remodeling of the building. But Saratoga Springs was not to become Las Vegas, and when casino gambling was outlawed in New York, Canfield sold The Casino to the city. A year later, in 1912, the Historical Society of Saratoga Springs took up permanent residence in these lavish quarters.

The collections of the Society concentrate largely upon Saratoga's own life and sprightly times and upon the Victorian age in which it flourished. The Hall of History traces the growth of the town from a frontier outpost to a grand resort and houses exhibits explaining the geological curiosity of the mineral springs. The Belter Room contains several splendid specimens of the work of John Henry Belter, the furniture maker whose elaborately carved rosewood chairs, tables, cupboards, and other pieces stand as the epitome of Victorian interior design.

On the third floor of The Casino, the historical society maintains the Walworth Memorial Museum, housing nineteenth-century furnishings and personal effects belonging to the family of Reuben H. Walworth, the last person to hold the office of chancellor of New York State.

The Casino, Congress Park, Saratoga Springs, NY 12866, (518) 584–6920, is open during June, September, and October from 10:00 A.M. to 4:00 P.M., Monday through Saturday; Sunday, 1:00 to 4:00 P.M. During July and August, The Casino is open daily from 9:30 A.M. to 4:30 P.M. From November 1 through Memorial Day, The Casino is open Wednesday through Sunday, 1:00 to 4:00 P.M. Admission is $2 for adults; $1.50 for students and senior citizens; and $.25 for children under 7.

Just outside Saratoga Springs are the **Petrified Gardens,** consisting of the exposed remains of a sea reef that thrived here beneath the Cambrian Sea 500 million years ago, give or take a year or two. Known since 1825 and properly identified in 1883, the "gardens" are the fossilized remains of cabbagelike plants related to modern algae. The reef they formed when alive teemed with trilobites, brachiopods, and rudimentary snails, fossils of some of which are visible among the plant fossils at this site. When the primordial seas receded, the vegetation was exposed, fossilized beneath layers of sediment, and eventually exposed again by the shearing action of the glaciers. These cryptozoöns, as they are called, are found elsewhere only at sites in northeast Asia and Western Australia.

At the Petrified Gardens, visitors can walk among these ancient plants, which can easily be distinguished by the untrained eye. Just look for gray, layered nodules, which look as if they might be broken and protruding sections of petrified cabbage. Stop along the way to admire a venerable though much younger specimen of vegetation, the "Iroquois Pine," one of the largest in the Adirondacks and estimated to be 300 years old. After you come in off the trail, you can buy fragments of cryptozoön at the gift shop.

Petrified Gardens, Petrified Gardens Road, off Route 29, Saratoga Springs, NY 12866, (518) 584–7102, is open daily, Memorial Day to Labor Day, 9:00 A.M. to 5:00 P.M. Closed Tuesdays and Wednesdays prior to July 1. Also closed when it rains. Admission is $2 for adults; $1.80 for students 13–18 and senior citizens; $1 for children 7–13.

Just north of Saratoga, where so much turn-of-the-century money was spent on the sporting life, is the town of Glens Falls, where a small fortune was instead disbursed on a remarkable collection of art. Glens Falls was the home of Charlotte Pruyn, heiress to a local paper fortune, who married Louis Fiske Hyde of Boston in 1901. In 1907 the Hydes returned to Glens Falls, and in 1912 they began building the Florentine villa which today houses the **Hyde Collection.** Influenced by the home-as-museum philosophy of the Boston Brahmin tastemaker Isabella Stewart Gardner, and with the help of connoisseurs such as Bernard Berenson, the Hydes filled their home with an eclectic and assiduously acquired collection of American and European art spanning five centuries.

The Hydes bought art with experts' eyes, concentrating not so much upon any individual period or school but upon the most expressive work of whichever painter or sculptor caught their attention. The end result was a collection that appears to have been amassed not by members of the upstate gentry but by a prince with a state treasury at his disposal. Of course, the Hydes were around at a time when the right things were on the market at prices that would make a modern collector weep, but they knew the right things when they saw them, and they spent their money with care.

Even before Louis Hyde's death in 1934, the Hydes had begun making plans to make their art collection accessible to the public someday. Employing curators to help round out her acquisitions (including the addition of twentieth-century work), Mrs. Hyde spent the next three decades working toward the day when her Adirondacks home would become an exquisite museum. Drawing upon a trust established by Mrs. Hyde in 1952, the Hyde Collection opened its doors to the public after her death, at the age of 96, in 1963.

And so it is that in Glens Falls, New York, you can enjoy paintings by Rubens, Van Dyck, Rembrandt, Tiepolo, Fragonard, Eakins, and Seurat. Here also are Botticelli's *Annunciation* and Degas' *Red Stockings.* There are nineteenth-century Americans, such as Homer and Whistler; and twentieth-century Europeans: Picasso, Cezanne, and Matisse. The collection, of course, is still housed in the Hydes' lovely villa, with its Renaissance Italian and eighteenth-century French furnishings. The museum's new education wing, designed by the renowned architect Edward Larrabee Barnes, links Hyde House to Mrs. Hyde's sister's home and provides new space in which to offer temporary exhibitions and a large variety of museum-related activities.

The Hyde Collection, 161 Warren Street, Glens Falls, NY 12801,

(518) 792–1761, recently reopened after extensive renovations. It is open Tuesday through Sunday, 10:00 A.M. to 5:00 P.M.; closed Mondays and national holidays. Admission is $3.50 for adults; $2.50 for students and senior citizens; free for children five and under. Everyone is admitted free on Sundays from 10:00 A.M. until 2:00 P.M. Fully accessible to the handicapped.

Of all the momentous phrases uttered or supposedly uttered throughout American history, one of the most memorable is Ethan Allen's thundering response to Captain Delaplace, the British commander of Fort Ticonderoga on Lake Champlain, when Delaplace asked Allen by what authority he was demanding the surrender of the fort. "I answered," wrote Allen later, " 'In the name of the great Jehovah, and the Continental Congress.' " The time was dawn, May 10, 1775.

Fort Ticonderoga, which stands on a promontory jutting into the southern end of Lake Champlain, is remembered by Americans mostly because of its brave capture that morning by Colonel Allen and his Green Mountain Boys, after which Henry Knox hauled its cannons overland for Washington to use in the siege of Boston. But the history of "Fort Ti" actually began twenty years earlier, when the French colonial administration in Quebec ordered the fort built as part of its southern defenses in the struggle against Great Britain for control of Canada. Called Fort Carillon by the French, it was originally built of earth and timbers, but it was later upgraded to the classic French fortress design with four pointed bastions offering an interlocking field of fire against attackers.

The attackers showed up in early July of 1758, in the form of 15,000 British and American colonial troops bent on taking the fort from the Marquis de Montcalm and his 3,500 French defenders. Montcalm held the British off and managed to withdraw most of his troops and blow up part of the fort before its eventual capture the following summer by Gen. Jeffrey Amherst. Amherst had the fort rebuilt, and the British maintained it with a light garrison until it was peacefully surrendered to Ethan Allen sixteen years later.

For two years Ticonderoga was an American fort, until British Gen. John Burgoyne forced its surrender during the southward march that ended in his defeat at Saratoga. A British garrison held it until October of 1777, when it was finally abandoned to the Americans and to time after a useful life of only twenty-two years. It was never again permanently manned and served only as a campsite for scouting and raiding parties throughout the remainder of the Revolution.

Fort Ticonderoga might be little more than an exhausted rubble quarry and a roadside marker if it had not been for the remarkable efforts of the Pell family to restore and maintain the historic structure over the past century and a half. William Ferris Pell of New York City bought the fort grounds in 1820, and in 1908 his descendant, Stephen Pell, began its complete reconstruction. (Stephen Pell's son, John Pell, presided over the Fort Ticonderoga Association until his death in 1988.) Consequently, visitors can walk through the stone buildings that replaced the original wooden structures of Fort Carillon, stride along the ramparts, and examine the barracks that once held a garrison of a hundred men. The South Barracks also house the fort's museum, containing exhibits of Indian and early military artifacts, maps and firearms, watercraft of the colonial and Revolutionary periods, and a collection of materials relating to the career of Ethan Allen. One of North America's best collections of cannons is also on display.

As a sidelight to a Fort Ticonderoga visit, drive to the nearby summit of Mt. Defiance, which figured in the British action against Ticonderoga's American defenders in 1777. Mt. Defiance offers especially fine views of Lake Champlain and its Vermont shoreline, on which yet another fortress site, Mt. Independence, is located. A short ferry ride beginning at the end of N.Y. Route 74 takes auto traffic to the Vermont side.

Fort Ticonderoga, Route 74, Ticonderoga, NY 12883, (518) 585–2821, is open daily from mid-May through mid-October. May, June, September, and October hours are 9:00 A.M. to 5:00 P.M.; July and August, 9:00 A.M. to 6:00 P.M. (Mt. Independence, in Vermont, is open daily, Wednesday through Sunday.) Admission is $5 for adults (14 and up); $3 for children 10–13; free for children under 10.

For some distance north of Ticonderoga, Lake Champlain remains narrow enough for a single military installation to have commanded both shores and governed the passage of ship traffic in the eighteenth century. This was the purpose of the fortifications that now lie in ruins at **Crown Point State Historic Site.**

At one time the site of a fur trading post and in the late 1600s the staging area for French raids on English settlements in New England and the Hudson Valley, Crown Point became the location of the French Fort St. Frederic, begun in 1734 and finished in 1737. The fort was designed as a stone citadel within outer walls, defended by twenty cannon and a garrison of 80 to 120 soldiers.

In 1755 Fort St. Frederic was targeted by the British as one of four strategic French forts to be taken as part of the final surge toward hegemony in North America. Four years later Gen. Jeffrey Amherst seized Crown Point and its fortress after it had been abandoned and partially destroyed by the French, who had used it as a fallback position after similarly abandoning Ticonderoga.

Amherst immediately ordered the construction of a much larger British fortress at Crown Point, which was substantially completed when the so-called French and Indian Wars ended in 1763. With hostilities ended, the fort began to deteriorate with neglect and was devastated by a 1773 fire. In 1775, a small British garrison there was captured by American militiamen under Seth Warner, after which Crown Point became the staging area for the abortive American attack on Canada. Serving for a while as the headquarters of an American patrol-boat force on Lake Champlain, the partially ruined facility was taken again by the British, who maintained a small force here until the end of the Revolution.

The survival of the walls, foundations, and partial structures that we see at Crown Point today is due to the 1910 conveyance of the property to the state by private owners who wished to see the ruins preserved. Stabilization work was carried out over the next half century, and in 1975 the area officially became a state historic site. The following year, the new visitor center and museum was opened. Highlights of the museum exhibits include artifacts uncovered at the site during extensive archaeological digs.

Crown Point State Historic Site, at the Lake Champlain Bridge 4 miles east of Routes 9N and 22, Crown Point, NY 12928, (518) 597–3666, is open May through October, Wednesday through Saturday, 10:00 A.M. to 5:00 P.M.; Sunday 1:00 to 5:00 P.M. Also open Memorial Day, Independence Day, and Labor Day. Open during the rest of the year by appointment only. Grounds are accessible all year. Admission is free.

Most museums seek to interpret a particular era, if history is their subject, or the artifacts surrounding a particular event or series of events. Not so the **Adirondack Museum** at Blue Mountain Lake in the heart of the mountain region. This institution's ambition, at which it has succeeded admirably, is the chronicling of the entire Adirondacks experience throughout the years in which the area has been known to man. Located on a peninsula surrounded by Blue Mountain Lake, the museum rambles through 22 separate exhibit buildings on a 30-acre compound and has been called the finest regional museum in the United States.

The thirty-three-year-old Adirondack Museum takes as its focus the ways in which people have related to this incomparable setting, and made their lives here, over the past two centuries. As befits an institution that began in an old hotel, the museum tells the story of how the Adirondacks were discovered by vacationists in the nineteenth century, especially after the 1892 completion of the first railroad through the region. Examples of nineteenth-century hotel and cabin rooms are shown, and a restored turn-of-the-century cottage houses a large collection of rustic "Adirondack Furniture," currently enjoying a revival among interior designers. There is an early-twentieth-century locomotive and a reproduction of an old-time stationmaster's office, as well as financier August Belmont's private railroad car *Oriental*—a reminder of the days when grand conveyances brought the very wealthy to even grander Adirondack mansions and clubs.

The workaday world of the Adirondacks is also recalled in mining, logging, and boat-building exhibits. The Adirondacks were (and still are) a great center for those who love canoes, and the museum possesses an excellent collection of handmade canoes and guideboats, including some of the lightweight masterpieces of nineteenth-century canoe-builder J. H. Rushton. The lovely sloop *Water Witch* is preserved under its own glass dome.

Special attention is given to what has been written and painted using Adirondacks subjects. The museum's picture galleries display the work of artists from the Hudson River School and later periods, and the library, open to researchers by appointment, contains more than eight thousand volumes on the region along with maps, manuscripts and unpublished records, and ephemera.

The Adirondack Museum, Route 28N/30, Blue Mountain Lake, NY 12812, (518) 352-7311/7312, is open daily from Memorial Day through mid-October, 9:30 A.M. to 5:30 P.M. Admission is charged.

Having been immersed in Adirondacks history and lore at Blue Mountain Lake, it is surprising to drive north and find a spot near Lake Placid and Saranac Lake whose principal connections are with events that occurred hundreds of miles from these mountains. Here, though, is the homestead and grave of the militant abolitionist John Brown, who was executed for his part in the 1859 raid on the U.S. arsenal at Harper's Ferry, Virginia. It is maintained today as the **John Brown Farm State Historic Site.**

Brown and several of his sons had organized their followers to stage the raid in the hope that the captured arms might be used to launch a war of liberation on behalf of black slaves in the

The John Brown Farm, Lake Placid

South. But his involvement in the abolitionist cause began years before the failed Harper's Ferry attack. His sons had homesteaded in Kansas during the period in the 1850s when the territory earned the name "Bloody Kansas" because of the struggle to decide whether it would be admitted to the Union as a slave or free state; Brown went to fight on the abolitionist side and took part in the desperate struggle at Osawatomie. But Brown wasn't a Kansan himself. Inasmuch as he had a permanent home during that turbulent period, it was his farm at North Elba, near Lake Placid. Here he had moved in 1849 to participate in a plan to settle free blacks in an agricultural community called Timbucto. The benevolent scheme hadn't worked, but Brown still considered North Elba home and had requested that he be buried there. Two of his sons, killed at Harper's Ferry, are also interred at the farm, as are several of his followers, whose remains were moved here in 1899.

The farmhouse at the John Brown Farm State Historic Site is open from late May through late October, Wednesday through Saturday, 10:00 A.M. to 5:00 P.M.; Sunday 1:00 to 5:00 P.M. Also open Memorial Day, Independence Day, and Labor Day. The grounds are open all year. Admission is free.

The Adirondacks, and in fact much of New York State, were once the territory of the Iroquois Confederation. Perhaps the most politically sophisticated of all the tribal groupings of North American Indians, the Iroquois actually comprised five distinct tribes—the Mohawks, Senecas, Onondagas, Oneidas, and Cayugas—who were later joined by the Tuscaroras to form the "six nations" of the confederation. The history and contemporary circumstances of the Iroquois are documented in the **Six Nations Indian Museum** near Onchiota, 14 miles north of Saranac Lake.

The cohesiveness of the five original nations of the Iroquois Confederation was already apparent at the time of the first European explorations of North America, although even greater solidarity among the tribes was no doubt fostered by their early perception of the French as a common enemy. This unfortunate turn in the history of the Quebec settlements began when Samuel de Champlain, leading an expedition of French explorers and Algonquin allies along Lake Champlain early in the seventeenth century, shot and killed an Iroquois chief. While this act of bravado may have further endeared him to the Algonquins, traditional enemies of the Iroquois, it made the Iroquois an implacable enemy of the French and an eventual ally of the British in their struggle for control of North America.

A visit to the Six Nations Museum, though, is a reminder that Iroquois culture and history have far deeper roots than are evident in the story of their involvement in the white man's conflicts. For centuries the Iroquois had been making their way through the forests of what is now New York State, building a society whose artifacts survive in the museum's collections: the elaborately beaded belts which told, in pictographic form, of the accomplishments of individuals and of the tribes; baskets and drums; clothing; jewelry; and even the sticks with which the Iroquois played the original version of the game we call lacrosse.

The Six Nations Museum also houses examples of the contemporary craftwork of Iroquois tribespeople, as well as models of typical Iroquois villages of the pre-European period.

The Six Nations Indian Museum, 1 mile out of Onchiota, NY 12968, (518) 891–0769, is open daily from July 1 through Labor Day, 9:30 A.M. to 6:00 P.M.; by appointment during May, June, September, and October. Admission is $1 for adults; $.50 for children.

To reach the museum, turn left 6 miles north of Vermontville on Route 3 north of Saranac Lake.

Once a part of the corridor used by trading and war parties in the days of the French and Indians, the area around Plattsburgh, on Lake Champlain, had settled into a peaceful mercantile existence by the end of the eighteenth century. It was in Plattsburgh that the **Kent-Delord House** was built in 1797 as a residence for William Bailey. Following several changes of ownership, the house was purchased in 1810 by Henry Delord, a refugee from the French Revolution who had prospered as a merchant and served in a number of local political offices in Peru, New York, before moving to Plattsburgh. Delord remodeled the house in the fashionable Federal style of the era and moved in in 1811, thus beginning more than a century of his family's residence here.

Just three years after the Delords moved into their new home, the War of 1812 came to Plattsburgh in the form of a southward thrust by British forces along Lake Champlain. The family—Delord, his wife Betsey, and daughter Frances—were even displaced during a week in September of 1814 when the British appropriated their house to billet troops. But the enemy was repelled later that month by the Delords' friend Commodore Thomas Macdonough in the Battle of Plattsburgh—the only major naval engagement ever fought on Lake Champlain.

Henry Delord was well connected. In addition to Commodore Macdonough, whose portrait hangs in the house today, the immigrant-turned-squire entertained such early-nineteenth-century notables as Gen. Winfield Scott, Col. Zebulon Pike (discoverer of Pike's Peak), and even President James Monroe. Several of the rooms in the house have been restored to their appearance during the days when these dignitaries paid their visits.

Successive members of the Delord family lived in the house until 1913. The last, Henry's granddaughter Fanny Webb Hall, who was a temperance activist and patent-medicine inventor, took up residence here in 1863 and remained until her death half a century later.

Aside from the wartime seizure of the house and the presidential visit, the story of the Kent-Delord House might be that of any home of a provincial bourgeois family during the nineteenth century. The difference, of course, is that this house has survived remarkably intact, having been purchased for use as a museum only eleven years after Fanny Hall's death. It offers a fine opportunity to see how an upper-middle-class family lived from the days just after the Revolution through the Victorian age and not incidentally houses a distinguished collection of American portrait art, including the work of John Singleton Copley, George Freeman, and Henry Inman.

The Kent-Delord House Museum, 17 Cumberland Avenue, Plattsburgh, NY 12901, (518) 561–1035, is open to guided tours Tuesday through Saturday at 10:00 A.M., 1:00 P.M., and 3:00 P.M., and by appointment. Admission is $2 for adults; $1 for students and senior citizens; and $.50 for children under 12.

When nations aren't running about occupying the homes of each other's citizens, they can accomplish quite a bit by acting in concert—as witness the **Saint Lawrence Seaway,** an example of construction and administrative cooperation between the United States and Canada that has linked the Atlantic Ocean with the ports of the Great Lakes for over three decades.

As the French fur traders of the seventeenth and eighteenth centuries knew, the Saint Lawrence River forms a natural highway between the farthest reaches of the Great Lakes and the tidal waters of the Gulf of Saint Lawrence. But modern commerce depends upon vessels with deeper drafts than the canoes of the *voyageurs,* and the rapids that characterize many sections of the Saint Lawrence between Lake Ontario and Montreal impeded all but the lightest and most maneuverable craft. Shippers and planners on both sides of the border were long aware of the need for a continuous deepwater channel to link the ocean with the Lakes, but it wasn't until the early 1950s, when it appeared that Canada would go ahead with its own section of the Seaway without United States participation, that the U.S. Congress finally passed legislation to authorize construction of the American portions of the project. The Saint Lawrence Seaway formally opened in 1959 and has since been operated by U.S. and Canadian commissions closely cooperating on maintenance, traffic regulation, and the setting of fees for passage.

The 2,342-mile distance that separates the open Atlantic from Duluth, on Lake Superior, also entails a vertical rise of 602 feet. Of the fifteen massive locks that enable ore and grain freighters and other cargo vessels to negotiate this passage, seven are located along the 190-mile stretch between Montreal and Lake Ontario. Two belong to the United States. These are the Bertrand H. Snell and Dwight D. Eisenhower locks, which are connected by a 3-mile canal at Massena, New York. Adjacent to the Eisenhower Lock is a Visitor Center, which affords excellent views of ships passing through the lock and also provides interpretive exhibits showing how the gates at either end of the structure take in and release water to lift and lower vessels passing through this section of the Seaway.

The Eisenhower Lock Visitor Center, off Route 37 in Massena, NY, (315) 764–3200, is open from May to October, roughly corresponding to the Seaway shipping season. For information on the times at which ships are expected to be passing through the lock, call (315) 769–2422.

New York State, as was mentioned in the introduction to this book, was somewhat of a staging area for America's westward expansion during the last century. It thus seems fitting that the greatest chronicler of the West in painting and sculpture was a New Yorker, who grew up in the town of Ogdensburg on the Saint Lawrence River halfway between Massena and Lake Ontario. His name was Frederic Remington, and a splendid collection of his work and personal effects is today housed in the **Frederic Remington Art Museum** in that community.

Born in 1861, Remington quit Yale at the age of nineteen and went west, where he spent five years garnering the experiences and images that would come across so powerfully in his paintings and sculpture. Success as an illustrator and later as a fine artist came after 1885; when Remington died suddenly following an operation in 1909, he was still riding the crest of his popularity. His wife moved from the Remington home in Connecticut in 1915 and settled in the artist's boyhood home of Ogdensburg, in a rented house that had been built in 1810. Mrs. Remington willed her husband's art collection, along with those of his own works in his possession at the time of his death, to the Ogdensburg Public Library, and five years after her own death, in 1923, the museum exhibiting this collection was opened in the house where she had lived.

The Remington works housed in the museum include fifteen bronzes, sixty oil paintings, ninety watercolors, and several hundred pen-and-ink sketches. Selections of works from his own collection, among them paintings by Charles Dana Gibson and the American impressionist Childe Hassam, are also on display. There is also a re-creation of Remington's last studio as it stood in Ridgefield, Connecticut, at the time of his death in 1909, and a collection of furnishings that reflect household tastes during the prime of Remington's life.

The Frederic Remington Art Museum, 303 Washington Street,

Ogdensburg, NY 13669, (315) 393–2425, is open from May 1 through October 31, Monday through Saturday, 10:00 A.M. to 5:00 P.M., Sunday, 1:00 to 5:00 P.M.; November 1 through April 30, Tuesday through Saturday, 10:00 A.M. to 5:00 P.M. Closed legal holidays.

Around the turn of the century, when Frederic Remington looked west for artistic inspiration, hotel magnate George C. Boldt turned instead to his native Germany. Boldt's creativity wasn't a matter of putting paint to canvas or molding bronze, however. He was out to build the 120-room **Boldt Castle,** Rhineland style, on one of the Thousand Islands in the Saint Lawrence River.

Boldt, who owned the Waldorf-Astoria in New York and the Bellevue-Stratford Hotel in Philadelphia, bought his island at the turn of the century from a man named Hart, but that isn't why it is named Heart Island. The name derives from the fact that the hotelier had the island physically reshaped into the configuration of a heart, as a token of devotion to his wife, Louise, for whom the entire project was to be a monumental expression of his love.

Construction of the six-story castle and its numerous outbuildings began in 1900. Boldt hired masons, woodcarvers, landscapers, and other craftsmen from all over the world to execute details ranging from terra-cotta wall inlays and roof tiles to Italian marble mantelpieces to a huge, opalescent glass dome. He planned and built a smaller castle as a temporary residence and eventual playhouse, a turreted private electrical generation station, extensive servants' quarters, and an underground tunnel for bringing supplies from the docks to the main house. A yacht house on nearby Wellesley Island protected Boldt's three yachts and houseboat, along with his racing launches; the 64-foot height of the main space would accommodate the standing masts of his sailing vessels. There were bowling alleys, a sauna, an indoor swimming pool—in short, it was to be the sort of place that would take years to finish and decades to enjoy.

But there weren't enough years left. Mrs. Boldt died suddenly in 1904, and George Boldt, heartbroken, wired his construction supervisors to stop all work. The walls and roof of the castle were by this time essentially finished, but crated fixtures such as mantels and statuary were left where they stood, and the bustling island fell silent. Boldt never again set foot in his empty castle, on which he had spent $2.5 million.

Boldt died in 1916, and two years later the island and its structures were purchased by Edward J. Noble, the inventor of Life

Savers candy. Noble and his heirs ran the deteriorating castle as a tourist attraction until 1962, when it was sold to the Treadway Inns Company; today, it belongs to the Thousand Islands Bridge Authority, which has stabilized the main buildings, performed long-deferred maintenance, and continued the program of tours and media presentations.

Boldt Castle, Heart Island, Alexandria Bay, NY 13607, (315) 482–2520 or 800–5ISLAND (in New York State), is accessible via water taxi from the upper and lower docks on James Street in Alexandria Bay, or to tour-boat patrons departing from both the American and Canadian shores. The Castle is open to visitors from late spring through early fall; for information, call ahead or write: 1000 Islands International Council, P.O. Box 400, Alexandria Bay, NY 13607. Admission is $3 for adults; $1.75 for children 6–12. Groups of twenty or more, senior citizens, and military personnel receive a discount.

If you find the most appealing aspect of George Boldt's heyday to be the sleek mahogany runabouts and graceful skiffs that plied the waters of the Thousand Islands and other Gilded Age resorts, make sure you find your way to the **Thousand Islands Shipyard Museum** in Clayton. The museum is a freshwater boatlover's dream, housing slender, mirror-finished launches (you wouldn't think of boarding one dressed in anything but white linen), antique canoes, distinctive Saint Lawrence River skiffs, handmade guide boats—more than 150 historic small craft in all.

The Shipyard Museum takes no sides in the eternal conflict between sailing purists and "stinkpotters," being broad enough in its philosophy to house a fine collection of antique outboard and inboard engines, including the oldest outboard known to exist. The one distinction rigidly adhered to pertains to construction material: All of the boats exhibited here are made of wood.

The Thousand Islands Shipyard Museum, 750 Mary Street, Clayton, NY 13624, (315) 686–4104, is open from mid-May to mid-October; call for specific hours. Admission is $4 for adults, with reduced rates for senior citizens, students, and children.

The international cooperation exemplified by the Saint Lawrence Seaway and the peaceful coexistence that allows pleasure craft to sail unimpeded along the boundary waters of the Saint Lawrence River and Lake Ontario are things that we take for granted today, but this state of affairs has hardly existed since time immemorial. Barely more than a century ago, the U.S. Navy kept an active installation at **Sackets Harbor,** on Lake Ontario's Henderson Bay, against the possibility of war with Canada. And during the War of 1812, this small lakeport actually did see combat between American and Anglo-Canadian forces.

At the time the war began, Sackets Harbor was not yet a flourishing American naval port and the site of a busy shipyard and supply depot. It was from here, in April of 1813, that the Americans launched their attack upon Toronto; a month later, the tables were turned when the depleted American garrison at the Harbor was beleaguered by a British attack upon the shipyard. The defenders repulsed the attack but lost much of their supplies to fire in the course of the struggle.

Today's visitor to Sackets Harbor can still see many of the facilities of the old naval base, including officers' homes and sites associated with the 1813 battle. Exhibits and interpretive audiovisual programs are housed in the 1817 Union Hotel, a handsome Federal-style structure acquired by the state of New York in 1972, shortly after the naval installation and its immediate surroundings became a state historic site.

Sackets Harbor Battlefield, 505 West Washington Street, Sackets Harbor, NY 13685, (315) 646–3634 or 646–3636, is open from late May to Labor Day, Wednesday through Saturday, from 10:00 A.M. to 5:00 P.M.; Sunday 1:00 to 5:00 P.M. Also open Memorial Day, Independence Day, and Labor Day. Grounds are open all year from 8:00 A.M. to sunset. Admission is free.

An even larger and more long-lived Lake Ontario military installation was located farther south, at Oswego. **Fort Ontario,** also a state historic site, dates back to the eighteenth-century struggles for control of the Great Lakes waged by Britain and France and saw use as a refugee processing center managed by the U.S. Army as recently as the 1940s. During the intervening years, this site at the mouth of the Oswego River has been defended beneath the flags of France, Britain, and the United States.

The first fort in this vicinity was built by the British in 1727. In 1755 the first Fort Ontario was built on the east shore of the Oswego, opposite the new Fort George. Both forts were destroyed by a French force under Montcalm only a year later, although the British were back by 1758 and built a larger and more permanent fort the following year. Instrumental as a staging area for British forces in the so-called French and Indian Wars, which ousted the French from Canada, Fort Ontario fell only briefly to the Americans during the Revolution and was not finally relinquished by the British until 1796, thirteen years after the formal cessation of hostilities.

Fort Ontario figured in the warfare along the Lake Ontario front during the War of 1812, when it was captured and destroyed (1814) by Gen. Gordon Drummond and his British forces. It was rebuilt in what was to become its final form between 1839 and 1844, during which time the American government feared that the anti-British rebellion in Upper Canada known as the Patriot War might involve the United States. Defenses were updated during the Civil War, when it was felt that the British, in keeping with their Confederate sympathies, might invade the northern states from Canada.

Fort Ontario was used as a training camp and hospital during World War I and again as a training facility during World War II. Between 1944 and 1946, refugees from German concentration camps were housed at the fort, which was finally decommissioned in the latter year.

In 1985 a major $300,000 restoration project of the fort buildings and their surroundings was completed by the state of New York. Among the tasks undertaken at this time were the replacement of the long-vanished original wooden retaining wall and revetments around the stone powder magazine, and a series of architectural digs which revealed shards of porcelain tableware and other eighteenth-century household artifacts and what is believed to be a part of the 1755 foundations of the English fort destroyed by Montcalm. In addition to the powder magazine, visitors can see 1840s barracks and officers' quarters, bastions and parapets assaulted by the British in 1814, and Civil War artillery casemates. Between July 1 and Labor Day, the costumed Fort Ontario Guard performs drills, fires cannon, and marches to the sounds of fifes and drums. Company F, 42nd U.S. Infantry, Veteran Reserve Corps reenacts daily life at the fort as it was in the summer of 1868.

Fort Ontario State Historic Site, off Route 104 in Oswego, NY 13126, (315) 343–4711, is open from mid-May through early fall (call for exact dates), Wednesday through Saturday and on Monday holidays, 10:00 A.M. to 5:00 P.M.; Sunday 1:00 to 5:00 P.M. Admission is charged.

The completion of our counterclockwise tour through the Adirondacks takes us east to a point just north of Utica, and the **Steuben Memorial State Historic Site.** Frederick von Steu-

Steuben Memorial, Remsen

ben was a Prussian officer who, at the age of forty-seven, migrated to the United States in 1777 to help drill the soldiers of the Continental Army. His first assignment was a challenging one: He was sent to the American winter encampment at Valley Forge, where morale was flagging and discipline, in the face of elemental hardships such as hunger and bitter cold, was virtually nonexistent.

As might be expected of a good Prussian officer, von Steuben rose to the occasion. Washington's troops at Valley Forge might not have had boots, but they learned how to march in file, as well as proceed through the other elements of classic military drill and perform effectively with the eighteenth-century frontline weapon of choice, the bayonet. The German emigré even found time to write a masterful treatise on military training, *Regulations for the Order and Discipline of the Troops of the United States.*

Having served as inspector general of the Continental Army until the end of the war, von Steuben was richly rewarded by the nation of which he had lately become a citizen. Among his other rewards was a New York State grant of 16,000 acres of land.

Allowed to pick his own site, he chose the area partially occupied today by the Steuben State Historic Site. He built a simple two-room log house here, having cleared some land for his own use, and began promoting settlement of much of the rest of the vast holding. But few newcomers had been attracted to this then-remote corner of the state by the time of his death in 1794; his legacy would be that of a man who marshalled the efforts of soliders, not civilians.

In 1936 the state erected a replica of von Steuben's log house on a site located within the 50 acres it had recently purchased as his memorial (the drillmaster is buried beneath an imposing monument not far from here, despite his wish that he lie in an unmarked grave). The cabin is open to visitors.

The Steuben Memorial State Historic Site, Starr Hill Road, Remsen, NY 13438, (315) 831-3737, is open from early May through Labor Day, Wednesday through Saturday and on Monday holidays, from 10:00 A.M. to 5:00 P.M.; Sunday, 1:00 to 5:00 P.M. Admission is free.

Off the Beaten Path in the Mohawk Valley

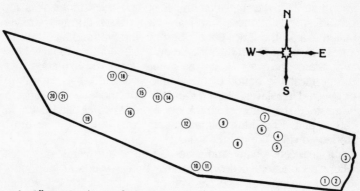

1. Albany Institute of History and Art
2. Schuyler Mansion
3. Waterford Village Sites
4. Schoharie Crossing
5. National Shrine of the North American Martyrs
6. Fonda National Shrine of Blessed Kater Tekakwitha
7. Fulton County Museum
8. Canajoharie Library and Art Gallery
9. Fort Klock Historic Restoration
10. Farmers' Museum
11. Fenimore House
12. Remington Firearms Museum
13. Munson Williams Proctor Institute
14. Children's Museum
15. Oriskany Battlefield
16. Musical Museum
17. Erie Canal Village
18. Revere Factory Store
19. Lorenzo State Historic Site
20. Erie Canal Museum
21. Everson Museum of Art

The Mohawk Valley

Drums Along the Mohawk . . . Leatherstocking . . . "I had a mule and her name was Sal/Fifteen miles on the Erie Canal" . . . The lore of the Mohawk Valley has long been a part of the national consciousness. The reasons are plain: The valley has been an important highway between the East and the Great Lakes for centuries, and countless Americans have passed through here via Indian trails, the Erie Canal, Commodore Vanderbilt's "Water Level Route" of the New York Central railroad, and today's New York State Thruway. Here was where Jesuit missionaries met their end at the hands of the Iroquois, where James Fenimore Cooper's Deerslayer stalked, and where those who were to homestead the Midwest struck out along a water-filled ditch, in barges pulled by draft animals. Surely, this is one of the most storied corridors of the republic.

Yet between Albany and Syracuse there are plenty of places where people settled down to make things—guns in Ilion; pots and pans in Rome; gloves, as you might suspect, in Gloversville. They nevertheless left no shortage of open land, as you can see when you crest one of the gently rolling hills in the dairy country near Cooperstown. If you are coming from the East, what you see here is a harbinger of the next fifteen hundred miles. It isn't prairie yet, but the land is opening up, and the horizon is growing more distant. This is where Midwestern vistas begin.

This chapter begins in Albany, very much an Eastern city and the capital of New York State. From here the direction followed is east to west, corresponding very closely to the route of the Mohawk River itself and, conveniently, the New York State Thruway.

The conventional, foursquare approach to Albany is by way of the public facade it presents—the massively beautiful and ornate State Capitol building, partly designed by H. H. Richardson, or the four monolithic, marble-clad state office towers so closely associated with the grandiose visions of the late Nelson Rockefeller. But in order to see a subtler side of the city and surrounding area and to learn more of its antecedents and historic persona than is revealed by those gargantuan examples of power frozen in masonry, visit the **Albany Institute of History and Art.** Descended from lyceums and art galleries that date back to 1791, the Institute has followed an acquisitions policy geared to the furnishings, household articles, folk art, and fine art of Albany and the upper Hudson River Valley.

Hudson River art, of course, means the Hudson River School, which is well represented here with works by painters such as Kensett, Cropsey, and Cole. But the Institute possesses fine examples of an even older regional genre, the sometimes-anonymous portraits of the Dutch burghers and their families who dictated the tone of Hudson Valley life during the seventeenth and eighteenth centuries. The Dutch in Holland, of course, had become the world masters of portraiture in the 1600s, as patrons and artists collaborated to compile a magnificent pictorial record of bourgeois life when the concept itself was still something new. It is fascinating to see how their New World counterparts worked a hundred years later. The experience is heightened by the Institute's collection of early Hudson Valley furniture and silver, which formed the day-to-day surroundings of the people in the portraits.

The Albany Institute of History and Art, 125 Washington Avenue., Albany, NY 12210, (518) 463–4478, is open Tuesday through Friday, 10:00 A.M. to 5:00 P.M.; Saturday and Sunday, noon to 5:00 P.M., and Thursday evenings until 8:00 P.M. The galleries are closed on Monday and certain holidays; call for specific information. Admission is by donation.

The Schuylers were among the earliest of the Dutch settlers of the upper Hudson Valley and were involved throughout the colonial period in trading, agriculture, land development, and local politics. The most renowned member of the family was Philip Schuyler (1733–1804), whose manorial home is today preserved as the **Schuyler Mansion State Historic Site.**

Although Albany has grown up around the mansion and deprived it of its once-rural hillside setting, it stands as a monument not only to its talented and versatile builder, but also to the best in eighteenth-century taste.

Philip Schuyler chose his then-125-acre homesite in 1760, by which time he had already served as a captain in the French and Indian Wars and married one of the neighboring van Rensselaers. He designed the mansion himself in the Georgian style, with rose-colored brick walls, graceful fenestration, and double-hipped roof (the awkward octagonal brick entry vestibule is an 1818 addition), and furnished it largely with purchases he made during a 1761–62 trip to England.

But like George Washington's Mount Vernon, the Schuyler Mansion was not to be a place of quiet retirement for its owner during his middle years. When the Revolution broke out, Schuyler became a delegate to the Continental Congress and was soon commissioned a major general in the new nation's army. Since his command was the Northern Department, he was able to operate out of his own Albany home—with the result that the parlors and drawing rooms of the Schuyler Mansion were visited by the likes of Washington, Franklin, Benedict Arnold, and Alexander Hamilton. Hamilton, in fact, wed Schuyler's daughter Elizabeth at the mansion in 1780.

A less willing guest at the Schuyler Mansion was British Gen. John Burgoyne, who was held captive here along with his officer staff after the American rout of his forces at the Battle of Saratoga.

Philip Schuyler was a prominent Federalist politician during the early years of the republic, serving as senator from New York in the first congress to convene under the federal constitution in 1789. He died in 1804, at which time his house and much of the family land in Albany were sold. Having been used as a private residence and later as an orphanage, the Schuyler Mansion was acquired by the state in 1912, restored, and opened to the public.

The Schuyler Mansion is as fine a place as New York State offers to learn about life as it was lived among the most fortunate levels of society in the mid-1700s. The house is an architectural gem, all the more impressive because of the amateur status of its architect (the soldier-statesman-planter-builder was not so rare a species in those days) and the excellent collection of colonial and Federal-period furnishings which it houses. Of particular note are the Hepplewhite pieces, Chinese export porcelain, and English glassware. Much of the home's contents were actually in the possession of the Schuyler family.

The Schuyler Mansion State Historic Site, 32 Catherine Street., Albany, NY 12202, (518) 434–0834, is open April through December, Wednesday through Saturday from 10:00 A.M. to 5:00 P.M.; Sunday, 1:00 to 5:00 P.M.; January through March, Saturday, 10:00 A.M. to 5:00 P.M., Sunday, 1:00 to 5:00 P.M. Also open on Memorial Day, Independence Day, and Labor Day. Group tours by reservation only. Admission is free.

One of Philip Schuyler's interests during his later years was the development of a canal and lock system in New York State. It was in the three decades after his death that canal building really hit its stride in the United States, turning formerly sleepy villages into canal boomtowns involved in the lucrative trade between New York City and points west. One such town is **Waterford,** located near Cohoes just upriver from Albany.

Founded by the Dutch as Halfmoon Point in the early 1620s at the point where the Mohawk River flows into the Hudson, Waterford was incorporated under its present name in 1794 and is today the oldest incorporated village in the United States. In 1799 it became the head of sloop navigation on the Hudson, but its glory days of commerce came later, in the 1820s, when the new Champlain and Erie canals made the town not merely a back-country terminus but an important way station and transfer point on a statewide transportation system.

Unfortunately for Waterford and many of its sister communities, not all major canal towns became major railroad towns after the iron horse ended the brief supremacy of the artificial waterways. Waterford did prosper as a small manufacturing center during the nineteenth century, however, and the legacy of this era is the village's lovely residential architecture, much of it in the regionally significant "Waterford" style characterized by Federal details and Dutch-inspired single-step gables. Such architectural distinctions have earned the village center a place on the National Register of Historic Places. The historic district is the subject of occasional tours given by the Village of Waterford Historical Commission; for information, contact the Commission's Historian and Preservation Officer, Garry F. Douglas, at 123 Fonda Road., Waterford, NY 12188.

From April through October in the village center at Erie Canal Lock Two, a series of outdoor exhibits details the history of the 1823 canal and the present-day barge canal. The panels trace the history of canal building in the state of New York and its impact on the development of the West. The murals depict two centuries of life on the canal and can be viewed daily from dawn until dusk. CanalFest, an annual event held on the second Saturday in May, celebrates the New York State Canal System and features boat rides, hayrides, a boat show, a craft fair, food and entertainment.

Waterford attractions outside the village center include the **Champlain Canal,** this section of which was dug in 1823 and which is still filled with water; the **Waterford Flight,** a series of five locks on the still-operating New York State Barge Canal, whose 169-foot total rise is the highest in the world; and the **Waterford Historical Museum and Cultural Center,** an 1830 structure in a late Federal-early Greek Revival style housing local art and history exhibits. Located at 2 Museum Lane, off Saratoga Avenue., Waterford, the Museum is open weekends from 2:00 to 4:00 P.M. Admission is free.

Schoharie Crossing, Fort Hunter

The Erie Canal and the feats of engineering that its building entailed are also the focus of **Schoharie Crossing State Historic Site,** farther up the Mohawk at Fort Hunter. Seven canal-related structures, dating from three periods of the waterway's construction or expansion, are preserved here and provided with interpretive displays that explain their use. Of particular interest are the original canal bed, circa 1825; a guardlock from the original canal; and the Schoharie Crossing itself, consisting of a massive arched aqueduct that carried the canal and its adjacent towpath across Schoharie Creek. This structure, dating from the enlargement of the canal in the 1840s, looks almost as if it might be a Roman ruin tucked into the hills of southern Europe. The Visitor Center has an exhibit on the Erie Canal and information on the site and surrounding area. The recently completed Putman's Canal Store, at Yankee Hill Lock #28 on Queen Anne's Road (about 2.2 miles east of the Visitor Center) was built during the 1850s and served as a store along the enlarged Erie Canal for many years. It now houses an exhibit on Erie Canal stores.

The old canal towpath at the site provides a pleasant place to walk, bicycle, or cross-country ski, stopping every so often to read the canal's story on the interpretive signposts along the way. At places on the towpath route, there are views of modern-day barge traffic on the Mohawk River, the depth of which in this area allows it to be used as a link in the New York State Barge Canal system.

Schoharie Crossing State Historic Site, Schoharie Street, Fort Hunter, New York 12069, (518) 829–7516, is open May 1 through October 31, and Memorial Day, Independence Day, and Labor Day, Wednesday through Saturday, 10:00 A.M. to 5:00 P.M.; Sunday, 1:00 to 5:00 P.M.. The grounds are open all year during daylight hours. Admission is free.

Long before there were canals or barges in this part of New York State, the waters of the Mohawk and its tributaries were plied by the canoes of the Iroquois. The Mohawk Valley was the heart of the empire of the five nations, one of which was the tribe that gave the river its name. Here, in what is today the town of Auriesville, stood the palisaded village of Mohawk longhouses called *Ossernenon* in the seventeenth century; here, in 1642, a raiding party of Indians returned with three French and twenty Huron captives in custody. Among the Frenchmen were a Jesuit priest, Isaac Jogues, and his lay assistant, Rene Goupil.

Enemies captured by the Iroquois—Hurons and Frenchmen were enemies by definition in those days—were lucky if they died quickly. Jogues and Goupil survived their tortures and were kept as slaves, although Goupil was tomahawked to death barely a month later when his attempt to teach a child the sign of the cross was interpreted as the casting of an evil spell. Jogues was rescued by the Dutch during a Mohawk trading foray to Fort Orange, and he returned to Europe and eventually Quebec. But he volunteered to go back to Ossernenon in May of 1646, as part of a group attempting to ratify a peace treaty with the Mohawks, and was captured near the village by a faction of the tribe favoring a continuation of hostilities. Both he and a lay companion, Jean Lalande, were murdered by tomahawk-wielding braves in October of that year. Canonized by the Roman Catholic Church in 1930 along with Goupil and five Jesuit missionaries martyred in

Canada, Jogues and Lalande are honored at the **National Shrine of the North American Martyrs** in Auriesville.

The shrine, which occupies the hilltop site of the original Mohawk village of Ossernenon amid 600 verdant acres, is maintained by the New York Province of the Society of Jesus, the same Jesuit order to which Issac Jogues belonged. Founded in 1885, the shrine accommodates approximately 200,000 visitors each year during a season lasting from the first Sunday in May to the last Sunday in October. Mass is celebrated in the vast "Coliseum," the central altar of which is built to suggest the palisades of a Mohawk village; there are also a Martyrs' Museum, rustic chapels, and a retreat house.

For information on the schedule of observances at the National Shrine of the North American Martyrs, Auriesville, NY 12016, call (518) 853–3033 or 829–7010.

The French Catholic missionaries working among the Indians in the seventeenth century were not without their successes. The most famous name among Mohawk converts of that era is that of Kateri Tekakwitha, the "Lily of the Mohawks," born at Ossernenon and baptized at what is now the village of Fonda, where the **Fonda National Shrine of Blessed Kateri Tekakwitha** is now located. Maintained by the Franciscan order of priests, the shrine commemorates the life of the saintly Indian girl who lived half of her life here, before removing to the community of converted Indians established by the French at Caughnawaga, near Montreal, where she died in 1680 at the age of twenty-four. (In 1980, on the tercentenary of her death, Pope John Paul II announced the beatification of Kateri Tekakwitha, which is the last step before canonization in the Catholic church.)

Aside from its religious connections, the Fonda site of the Tekakwitha shrine is interesting because of its identification by archaeologists as the location of a Mohawk village, also called Caughnawaga. Seven years of careful and extensive excavations during the 1950s revealed the exact locations of the individual longhouses that lay within the walls of the village, as well as the course of the walls themselves. Stakes mark the sites of both houses and walls. Artifacts dug from the village site are exhibited in the shrine's Mohawk-Caughnawaga Museum, located on the ground floor of a Revolutionary-era Dutch barn which now serves as a chapel. Indian items from elsewhere in New York State and throughout the United States are also part of the museum's collections.

The Fonda National Shrine of Blessed Kateri Tekakwitha, off Route 5, Fonda, NY 12068, (518) 853–3646, is open daily, May through October. Museum admission is free. For information on masses and other religious observances, call the Conventual Franciscan Fathers at the above number.

Just north of Fonda and nearby Johnstown is Gloversville, home of the **Fulton County Museum.** Gloversville was originally called Kingsborough, but the townspeople adopted the present name in 1828 in homage to the linchpin of the local economy in those days—tanning and glove making. It is the glove industry that provides the Fulton County Museum with its most interesting exhibits, housed in the Glove and Leather Room. Here is the state's only glove-manufacturing display—a complete small glove factory of the last century, donated to the museum and reassembled in its original working format. Also on display are a mural chronicling the growth of the glove industry against a background of contemporary artifacts, and the "worlds largest glove," an all-leather monstrosity standing a good 5 feet high.

There is also a Weaving Room that demonstrates the technique from raw flax to the finished product; an Old Country Kitchen; a nineteenth-century Lady's Room, complete with costumes and cosmetics; a Country Store; an old-time Candy Store; an Early Farm display; and an old-time Country Schoolroom. Don't miss the Indian Artifact exhibit on the first floor.

The Fulton County Museum, 237 Kingsboro Avenue., Gloversville, NY 12078, (518) 725–2203, is open during April, May, and June, Tuesday through Saturday, noon to 4:00 P.M.; July and August, Tuesday through Saturday, 10:00 A.M. to 4:00 P.M., and Sunday, noon to 4:00 P.M. Call for hours after September 1 and for dates of winter closing. Admission is free.

Fate plays a capricious hand in deciding which industries a town will be noted for. Gloversville got gloves; Canajoharie, our next stop along the Mohawk, got chewing gum—specifically, the Beech-Nut Packing Company, of which town native Bartlett Arkell was president in the 1920s. Because of Mr. Arkell and his success in business, Canajoharie also came into possession of the finest independent art gallery of any municipality its size in the United States—the **Canajoharie Library and Art Gallery.**

Arkell's beneficence to his hometown began with his donation of a new library in 1924. Two years later he donated the funds to build an art-gallery wing on the library, and over the next few years he gave the community the magnificent collection of paintings that forms the bulk of the gallery's present holdings. In 1964 yet another wing was added, paid for by the Arkell Hall Foundation.

This institution has not merely become an art gallery with a library attached, but an art gallery with a small town attached. The roster of American painters exhibited here is astounding, totally out of scale with what you would expect at a Thruway exit between Albany and Utica. The Hudson River School is represented by Albert Bierstadt *(El Capitan),* John Kensett, and Thomas Doughty. There is a Gilbert Stuart portrait of George Washington. The Winslow Homer collection is the third largest in the United States; a new gallery now houses this collection. The eighteenth century is represented by John Singleton Copley; the nineteenth by luminaries such as Thomas Eakins, George Inness *(Rainbow),* and James McNeil Whistler*(On the Thames).* Among twentieth-century painters there are Charles Burchfield, Reginald Marsh, and the painters of the Ash Can School; N. C. Wyeth and his son Andrew *(February 2nd);* Edward Hopper, Thomas Hart Benton, and even Grandma Moses. There is also a Frederic Remington bronze, *Bronco Buster.* Add a collection of eighty Korean and Japanese ceramics, the gift of the late Col. John Fox, and you have all the more reason—as if more were needed—to regard Canajoharie as a destination in itself rather than a stop along the way.

The Canajoharie Library and Art Gallery, 2 Erie Boulevard, Canajoharie, NY 13317, (518) 673-2314, is open Monday through Friday, from 9:30 A.M. to 4:45 P.M., Thursday evening until 8:30. Saturday hours are from 9:30 A.M. to 1:30 P.M. Admission is free.

Art played little part in the life of the Mohawk Valley in the year 1750, when Johannes Klock built the farmhouse-fortress preserved today as the **Fort Klock Historic Restoration.** Located above the river at Saint Johnsville, Fort Klock is a reminder that the building of stout-walled outposts capable of being held defensively was by no means confined to the "wild west" of the late 1800s. In 1750 the Mohawk Valley *was* the wild west, and a man like Klock found it necessary to build a home that could serve just as easily as a fortress. The enemy was not only the Indians but also the French; and twenty-five years later the valley would become a theater of warfare involving American rebels, Tories, British regulars, and mercenary Indians.

Like his neighbors at scattered sites along the river, Johannes Klock engaged in fur trading and farming. Canoes and bateaux could tie up in the cove just below the house, yet the building itself stood on high enough ground and at a sufficient distance from the river to make it easily defensible should the water of the Mohawk bring foes rather than friendly traders. The stone walls of Fort Klock are almost 2 feet thick and are dotted with "loopholes" that enable inhabitants to fire muskets from protected positions within.

Johannes Klock's descendant John Klock lived here during the Revolution, in which he fought on the American side. The war was hard on the area: 700 homes were burned, and a third of the population of the valley, some 10,000 people, left for the safety of Canada. Those who remained, and who survived the hostilities, often had the strong walls of structures such as Fort Klock to thank for their security.

Now restored and protected as a registered National Historic Landmark, Fort Klock and its outbuildings tell a good part of the story of the Mohawk Valley in the eighteenth century—a time when the hardships of homesteading were made even more difficult by the constant threat of the musket, the tomahawk, and the torch.

Fort Klock Historic Restoration, Route 5, Saint Johnsville, NY 13452, (518) 568-7779, is open from mid-May through mid-October, Tuesday through Sunday, 9:00 A.M. to 5:00 P.M. Admission is $1 for adults. $.50 for children 10–15. Group tours welcome; by appointment only.

One of the best known of all Mohawk Valley towns (it's actually a good deal south of the river, on Otsego Lake) is Cooperstown, named for the family of novelist James Fenimore Cooper and synonymous with ultimate achievement in America's national pastime. The Baseball Hall of Fame and Museum is what brings most visitors to Cooperstown—but when they get there, they are often surprised to find that the community also harbors an equally engaging museum dedicated to the experience of rural life in days gone by. This is the **Farmers' Museum,** part of the New York State Historical Association's Cooperstown holdings that also include **Fenimore House,** which presents collections of American folk and academic art and James Fenimore Cooper memorabilia.

The particular focus of the Farmers' Museum is the period between the American Revolution and the Civil War, when most Americans still lived in rural areas. None of the tasks associated with farming and homemaking had yet been subjected to mechanization in those days, and country people had to rely not only upon their own ingenuity and capacity for hard work but upon a small-scale infrastructure of blacksmiths, weavers, and other craftspersons. The museum's "Village Crossroads" gathers these and other town fixtures together in a community of more than a dozen early-nineteenth-century buildings, all built within a hundred miles of Cooperstown and moved here as life-size, working exhibits. The village includes a blacksmith's shop, church, tavern, country store, one-room schoolhouse, lawyer's and doctor's offices, print shop, druggist's shop, cattle barn, and homestead. Museum personnel work as did the craftspeople they represent, making horseshoes or brooms, or setting type by hand, or cooking at an open hearth, all the while ready to answer visitors' questions and explain the day-to-day life of country towns a century and a half ago.

Yet these were agricultural communities, and whatever else had to be done, farm work itself was most important. The "Living Historical Farm" at the museum demonstrates the farming practices of the day; there are cattle, a cornfield, and even a flock of sheep. The Main Barn, which houses the museum's principal indoor exhibits, offers displays of farm, craft, and household implements of the era.

Annual events held at the museum include draft horse demonstrations, old-time Fourth of July celebrations, a Harvest Festival, and a Candlelight Evening at Christmastime.

The Farmers' Museum and Fenimore House (headquarters of the New York State Historical Association), Cooperstown, NY, (607) 547–2593 for Museum, 547–2533 for Fenimore House, are open from May 1 through October 31 daily, 9:00 A.M. to 6:00 P.M.; call regarding off-season schedules. Admission to the Museum is $6 for adults; $2.50 for children 7–15; Fenimore House admission is $5 for adults; $2 for children. Inquire about discount tickets for admission to both attractions or to all three (Museum, Fenimore House, and Baseball Hall of Fame).

It was an environment very much like the one depicted at the Farmers' Museum's Village Crossroads that produced one of the great American toolmakers, inasmuch as dependable firearms were indispensable tools of frontier life and westward expansion. In 1816 Eliphalet Remington was twenty-four years old and in need of a new rifle. He made a barrel at his father's village forge and then walked into the Mohawk Valley town of Ilion to have it rifled (rifling is the series of twisting grooves inside a gun barrel, which give the bullet spin—and therefore accuracy—and distin-

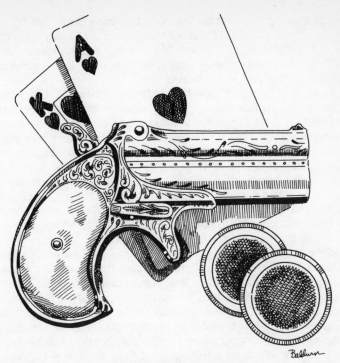

Antique Double Derringer

guish it from the smoothbore muskets of earlier days). He may not have known it then, but gun-making was to be his life's work and the Remington Arms Company his creation. You can learn the history of America's oldest gun-maker at the **Remington Firearms Museum** in Ilion, which houses an impressive collection of rifles, shotguns, and handguns dating back to Eliphalet Remington's earliest flintlocks. Here are examples of the first successful breech-loading rifles, for which Remington held the initial 1864 patents; rare presentation-grade guns; and company firsts including bolt-action and pump rifles, autoloading rifles and shotguns, and the Model 32 over-and-under shotgun of 1932.

Other displays include explanations of how firearms are built today, advertising posters and other firearms ephemera, and even antique Remington typewriters—yes, it was the same company. Changing exhibitions in the museum's gallery spotlight items of special interest, such as guns that belonged to famous people.

The Remington Firearms Museum, Catherine Street, off Route 5S, Ilion, NY 13357, (315) 894–9961, is open Monday through Saturday, 9:00 A.M. to 4:00 P.M. From May through October, the museum is also open on Sunday, 1:00 to 4:30 P.M. It is accessible to the handicapped. Admission is free.

From Ilion, it's just a short hop down the Thruway to Utica and a pair of worthwhile museums. The **Munson Williams Proctor Institute** is the sort of thing small cities do well, given farsighted founders and the right endowment. The Institute is a multifaceted operation that places a good deal of emphasis on community accessibility and service, with free group tours, a speakers' bureau, and children's art programs, as well as free admission and a modestly priced performing arts series (performances take place at the nearby Stanley Performing Arts Center). But you don't have to be a Utica resident to enjoy the major holdings, which include a collection of paintings strong in nineteenth-century genre work and the Hudson River School, as well as moderns such as Calder, Picasso, Kandinsky, and Pollock; comprehensive art and music libraries; a sculpture garden; and even a children's room where patrons can leave their kids for supervised play while they enjoy the museum. Also on the grounds of the Institute is Fountain Elms, a beautifully restored 1850 home in the Italianate Victorian style, which was once the home of the philanthropic Proctor family. Four period rooms on the ground floor exemplify Victorian tastes, while an upstairs gallery at Fountain Elms contains displays of furniture and household implements. At Christmastime, the house is resplendent with Victorian ornamentation.

The Munson Williams Proctor Institute, 310 Genesee Street, Utica, NY 13502, (315) 797–0000, is open Tuesday through Saturday, 10:00 A.M. to 5:00 P.M.; Sunday, 1:00 to 5:00 P.M. Hours apply to both the art galleries and Fountain Elms. Admission to both the museum and the house is free.

Having retrieved your little ones from the children's room at the Institute, take them next to a museum of their own. Utica's **Children's Museum** is now the largest such institution just for kids in the state, outside New York City, having grown like Topsy in the quarter-century since its founding by the city's Junior League. Since 1980 it has occupied its own five-story, 30,000-square-foot building, which it keeps chock full of participatory and "hands-on" exhibits concentrating on natural history, the history of central New York State, and technology. Installations, designed for children ages 2–12 and their families, include a Dino

Den, (dinosaur books, puzzles, models, etc.), Childspace, (creative play area for preschoolers), Iroquois longhouse and artifacts, a natural-history center, bubbles (a play area with a giant bubble-making device), an architecture area, and a dress-up area. The Museum also offers special exhibitions on a monthly basis and special programs for children and their families on Saturdays beginning at 2:00 P.M., from October through July. Portions of the permanent Railroad Exhibit, which includes a Sante Fe dining car and diesel locomotive, are on display next to the Museum.

The Children's Museum, 311 Main Street, Utica, NY 13501, (315) 724–6128, is open between July 4 and Labor Day, Tuesday through Saturday 10:00 A.M. to 4:30 P.M.; Sunday, 1:30 to 4:30 P.M. During the rest of the year, hours are 12:30 to 4:30 P.M., Wednesday through Friday; Saturday, 10:00 A.M. to 4:30 P.M.; The museum is closed on most major holidays. Admission is $1.50 for adults and children over 3; members and infants free. The maximum family charge is $7.50.

Like many eighteenth-century conflicts, the War for American Independence was not the sort of all-out bloodbath to which we have become inured in the century that gave us Verdun and Stalingrad. But given the right ingredients—a British ambush, tomahawk-wielding Iroquois mercenaries, a patriot force that fought like cornered wolverines—a summer day in the Mohawk Valley could turn nasty indeed. Such is the story told at the **Oriskany Battlefield State Historic Site.**

The British strategy for the summer of 1777 called for dividing the Middle Atlantic colonies from the New England colonies via a three-pronged attack in New York. Gen. John Burgoyne, as we saw earlier in this book, was to descend on the Hudson Valley from Canada, while another of His Majesty's armies was to head north from New York. The central thrust of this three-way attack was to be made by Col. (temporarily Brig. Gen.) Barry St. Leger, who would attack Albany from Lake Ontario by way of the Mohawk Valley.

The northward attack from New York City was never made, and we saw what happened to Burgoyne at Saratoga. What of St. Leger? His army bogged down at the siege of western New York's Fort Stanwix, which the patriot defenders held much more tenaciously than the British had expected. To make matters worse for the attackers, a relief party of 800 men and boys under the Continental Army's Gen. Nicholas Herkimer had begun to march toward Fort Stanwix in hopes of lifting the siege. St. Leger decided to seize the initiative and meet the fort's would-be rescuers before they could reach his main position. To this end, he dispatched two Tory leaders, Sir John Johnson and Col. John Butler, to lead a contingent of Loyalists and Iroquois warriors (under chief Joseph Brant) to intercept Herkimer's force in ambush.

The Tories and Indians fell upon Herkimer and his men as they emerged from a ravine near Oriskany on August 6, 1777. The first volley brought down Gen. Herkimer, who, with a mortal musket-ball wound in his leg, continued to shout orders to his troops. Both sides closed in too quickly for successive musket volleys to be exchanged by orderly lines of soldiers in classic eighteenth-century fashion, and the fighting quickly descended to hand-to-hand grappling with bayonets and tomahawks. The patriots fought fiercely—so fiercely that the Indians gave up the field, followed soon after by the Tories and British regulars, on whose behalf they had joined the fray. The British survivors retreated to Fort Stanwix, where their absence during the Oriskany battle had done St. Leger's cause no good. The siege of the fort was abandoned, and the British returned to Canada. Their Mohawk Valley thrust had been thwarted, thanks largely to the bravery of Gen. Herkimer—dead of his wounds within a few days after the battle—and his militia of farmers and their sons.

This bloodiest of American Revolutionary battles is commemorated at the Oriskany site by an audiovisual show at the visitor center, by guided walking tours of the actual battlefield, and by a memorial obelisk built in 1884.

Oriskany Battlefield State Historic Site, Route 69, 2 miles west of Oriskany, NY 13424, (315) 768–7224, is open from early May through Labor Day, Wednesday through Saturday and Monday holidays, 9:00 A.M. to 5:00 P.M.; Sunday, 1:00 to 5:00 P.M. An anniversary celebration is held every August 6.

On a lighter note . . . just to the southwest of Oriskany and Utica, in the small town of Deansboro, is the extraordinary **Musical Museum** operated by the Sanders family since 1948. The very idea of such a place might be enough to keep a layperson in the fast lane on the Thruway, but don't make that mistake. This is *not* a collection of old oboes in glass cases but a seventeen-room agglomeration of the kinds of instruments anyone can play: player pianos, ancient jukeboxes, harmoniums and melodeons, and just about every sort of early phonograph and music box. Anyone *can* play the exhibits—literally. Restored to operating condition, most of the musical contraptions at the museum are there for the cranking, pumping, or whatever else is required of the curious visitor to make sound come out.

The Musical Museum began when Hardie Sanders realized that his hobby of collecting mechanical musical paraphernalia was threatening to take over every inch of space in his home. Today, the museum is run by his son Arthur, who, like his father, is dedicated not only to finding old and rare instruments but to restoring them so that they can be played.

Among the exhibits at the museum are an incredible mechanical violin player built in 1912 (no computers here; just a complicated system of motors, switches, and magnets), the coin-operated player pianos that were the first "jukeboxes," an 1,800-pound Wurlitzer band organ that reproduces the sound of an entire twenty-piece band, and even a compressed-air calliope. (The original steam calliopes were enormous, cumbersome affairs with their own boilers; only seventy-five or so ever operated in the United States.) Perhaps the most fascinating device on exhibit is a circa 1910 German Welte-Mignon automatic piano, which was designed to record and play back piano performances with the exact nuances of style and expression that characterized the "recording session." Thus we can hear Saint-Saens or Paderewski actually playing, not through the medium of a phonograph disc but through the coding of holes on a paper roll.

Many of the instruments in the museum's collection have been recorded, and albums are available for purchase on the premises. In addition, the museum operates a repair service for antique instruments of the type they display and even a sideline operation specializing in antique lamps, lamp parts, and repairs.

The Musical Museum, Route 12B, Deansboro, NY 13328, (315) 841–8774, is open daily April 1 through December 31, 10:00 A.M. to 4:00 P.M. Admission is $3.50 for adults; $2.50 for children 6–12; free for children under 12.

If a parlor organ can carry you back in time, think of what a ride on a horse-drawn canal boat will do. That was the original idea behind the **Erie Canal Village,** which opened in Rome in 1973 near the site where the first spadeful of dirt for the Erie Canal was dug on Independence Day in 1817.

It's difficult for us to make modern-day comparisons with the Erie Canal in terms of national pride, public excitement, and the sense of heroic accomplishment that the project inspired in the new republic. The space program? Our pride in U.S. space accomplishments is necessarily more vicarious, since few of us are going up there ourselves. But imagine building the first commercial pathway into the heart of the continent—a level water-road that would replace the treacherous footpaths and wagon routes that had stifled trade and settlement in earlier years. The short-lived canal era may only have been a prologue to the age of the railroad—but in the 1820s, New Yorkers felt the Erie Canal was one of the wonders of the world.

The *Chief Engineer,* which keeps to a regular schedule of forty-five-minute trips on the restored section of the original canal at the Village, was built of Mohawk Valley oak to the same specifications as the passenger-carrying packet boats of the canal's early years. The core attraction of the village, it has since been joined by a narrow-gauge, one-half scale steam locomotive, the *Edward Nolan,* and the Harden Carriage Museum, which comprises a varied collection of horse-drawn vehicles used on roads and snow. Other buildings in the Village—nearly all of which are more than a hundred years old and were moved here from other communities in the area—include a tavern, church, smithy, settler's house, barn, and the New York State Museum of Cheese. The Erie Canal museum, housed in a building of newer construction, houses exhibits explaining the technological and social importance of the Erie Canal. Fort Bull, dating from the French and Indian Wars, is also on the premises.

Erie Canal Village, Routes 49 and 46, Rome, NY 13440, (315) 336–6000, is open from mid-May through mid-September, daily, 9:30 A.M. to 5:00 P.M. Admission is charged. Boat rides are an additional $1 per person.

If a visit to the Erie Canal Village or the Fort Stanwix National Monument has brought you to Rome, stop in at the **Revere Factory Store.** The store offers terrific bargains on slightly irregular and factory-closeout items from their standard line of copper-clad stainless steel, as well as aluminum-slab stainless steel and copper-slab stainless steel. Saucepans and saucepots of up to 20-quart capacity are available, as are skillets up to 12 inches in diameter. They also carry Corning Ware and other selected kitchen equipment.

The Revere Factory Store, 137 Liberty Plaza, Rome, NY 13440, (315) 338–2223, is open Monday through Saturday, 9:00 A.M. to 5:00 P.M.

Back before the Erie Canal was built, years before anyone thought of putting a copper bottom on a steel pot, this part of New York State was the western frontier, ripe for settlement, agriculture, and the development of manufacturing. During those first

Lorenzo, Cazenovia

decades of American independence, land development companies operated much as they had in colonial times, securing rights
to vast sections of virgin territory and undertaking to bring in
settlers and get them started. (Years later, the big railroad companies would follow the same practice in Canada and the United
States.) One such outfit was the Holland Land Company, which in
1790 sent its young agent, John Lincklaen, to America to scout
investment possibilities. Two years later he reached the area
around Cazenovia Lake, between present-day Rome and Syracuse, and his enthusiasm for the area's prospects led his firm to
invest in 120,000 acres here. A village, farms, and small businesses soon thrived, with Lincklaen remaining in a patriarchal
and entrepreneurial role that demanded the establishment of a
comfortable family seat. The result was Lincklaen's 1807 building
of his magnificent Federal mansion, Lorenzo, today preserved at
the **Lorenzo State Historic Site.**

The little fiefdom of Lorenzo offers an instructive glimpse into why New York is called the "Empire State." Lincklaen and the descendants of his adopted family, who lived here until 1968 (the same year that the house, with its contents, was deeded to the state), were involved with many of the enterprises that led to the state's phenomenal growth during the nineteenth century—road building, canals, railroads, and industrial development.

Lorenzo itself is rich in Federal-era furnishings and the accumulated possessions of a century and a half of Lincklaens. It is surrounded by 20 acres of lawns and formal gardens, amidst which is restored carriage house that holds a collection of horse-drawn vehicles used over the years on the roads around the estate, and an introductory exhibition on the history of the property.

Lorenzo State Historic Site, Route 13, Cazenovia, NY 13035, (315) 655–3200, is open Memorial Day through Labor Day, Wednesday through Saturday and on Monday holidays, 10:00 A.M. to 5:00 P.M.; Sunday, 1:00 to 5:00 P.M. The grounds are open all year, 8:00 A.M. until dusk. Admission is free, although as of this writing the management is considering a charge.

A swamp northwest of Cazenovia was destined for an even grander future as the nineteenth century began. This was the site of Syracuse, which would be lifted to prominence by the salt industry and the Erie Canal and which today contains the last of the "weighlock" buildings that once dotted the waterway. Built in 1850 in Greek Revival style, this weigh station for canal boats today houses the **Erie Canal Museum.**

How did they weigh canal boats? The procedure used here can be more clearly understood if you begin by envisioning the Erie Canal flowing along the present route of Erie Boulevard. Boats were towed into a "weighlock chamber" on the open, canal-side section of the building, after which lock gates were closed at the front and the rear. When the water was drained out of the chamber, the boat came to rest on a wooden cradle that constituted the bed of an enormous scale. The boat was weighed, tolls were assessed accordingly, and water was readmitted to the chamber to float the boat along its way when the gates were reopened. The procedure was cumbersome, but essentially simple.

The Weighlock Building was restored in 1985 to house the twenty-five-year-old museum, which expanded and reorganized its exhibits. One project was the construction of a 65-foot replica of a canal boat within the building's walls. The *Frank Buchanan*

Thomson, as the new boat has been named after a late museum director, offers a look at a typical Erie Canal vessel's crew quarters, immigrant accommodations, and cargo storage. Immigration along the canal is a special focus of the museum's exhibits, particularly with regard to its effects upon Syracuse. The museum experience also includes an audiovisual program on the canal's history and significance, a hands-on display of canal equipment, and explanations of the engineering involved in connecting Albany and Buffalo by means of a 363-mile artificial waterway with eighty-three locks and eighteen aqueducts. The job wasn't easy, but the result was the longest and most successful canal in the world.

The Erie Canal Museum, 318 Erie Boulevard East, Syracuse, NY 13202, (315) 471–0593, is open Tuesday through Sunday, 10:00 A.M. to 5:00 P.M. Admission is $1 for adults; $.50 for children; free to all on Tuesdays.

Having passed through the stages from swamp to canal boomtown to major commercial and industrial center by the end of the nineteenth century, Syracuse was ready for an art museum. The idea for the institution that was to become today's **Everson Museum of Art** came from George Fisk Comfort, a lion of the American art establishment who had been instrumental in establishing New York City's Metropolitan Museum and served as founder and dean of the College of Fine Arts at Syracuse University. Comfort organized the museum as the Syracuse Museum of Fine Arts, and in 1900 the first exhibition took place. A progressive policy toward acquisitions was in evidence even at that early date, with the initial show featuring, among older and more recognized masters, the work of impressionists such as Monet, Sisley, and Pissarro. The policy of acquiring and showing contemporary painters and sculptors continued under Comfort and his successors, along with a distinct inclination toward American artists.

Renamed the Everson Museum in 1959 following a large bequest from the estate of Syracuse philanthropist Helen Everson, the museum moved in 1968 into its present quarters, a massive, modernist concrete structure by I. M. Pei that was the architect's first museum building. Its three exhibition levels contain four galleries and a 50-foot-square, two-story sculpture court.

What to look for at the Everson? The emphasis is heavily American, particularly with regard to ceramics. The museum's Syracuse China Center for the Study of American Ceramics houses the nation's premier collection in this field, with holdings dating from A.D. 1000 to the present. Here are pre-Columbian native American vessels; colonial and nineteenth-century pieces; and contemporary functional and art pottery, as well as some 1,200 examples of ceramic craftsmanship from cultures outside the Western Hemisphere.

The Everson's holdings also include anonymous colonial portraits (and one very famous and not so anonymous one of George Washington); nineteenth-century genre and luminist painters; and twentieth-century names such as Robert Henri, John Sloan, Grandma Moses, Maxfield Parrish, Reginald Marsh, and Grant Wood. The museum possesses a good graphic art collection and a small but comprehensive photography section.

The Everson holds some thirty temporary exhibitions each year, featuring work by modern masters and emerging contemporary artists as well as more traditional themes. In these special shows, too, the emphasis is on American work. The museum also includes a gift gallery and a lunch gallery.

The Everson Museum of Art, 401 Harrison Street, Syracuse, NY 13202, (315) 474–6064, is open Tuesday through Friday, noon to 5:00 P.M.; Saturday, 10:00 A.M. to 5:00 P.M.; Sunday, noon to 5:00 P.M. Admission is free, although a suggested donation of $2 is welcome.

Off the Beaten Path in the Southern Tier

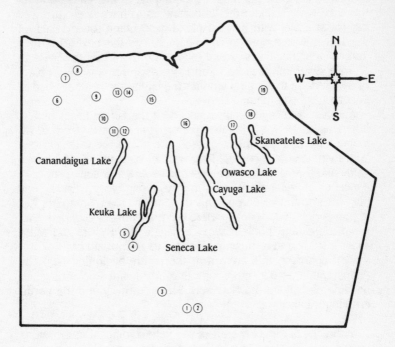

1. Mark Twain Study
2. National Soaring Museum
3. The Rockwell Museum
4. Glenn H. Curtiss Museum
5. The Wine and Grape Museum of Greyton H. Taylor
6. Genesee Country Village and Museum
7. Victorian Doll Museum
8. Margaret Woodbury Strong Museum
9. Valentown Museum
10. AWA Electronic Communications Museum
11. Granger Homestead and Carriage Museum
12. Sonnenberg Gardens
13. Hill Cumorah
14. Alling Coverlet Museum and William Phelps General Store Museum
15. Hoffman Clock Museum
16. Memorial Day Museum
17. Cayuga Museum
18. The Krebs Restaurant
19. Beaver Lake Nature Center

The Southern Tier

Here, between New York's "northern seaboard" along Lake Ontario and the Pennsylvania border, lies the region that many visitors consider to be the most beautiful part of the state. South of the Lake Ontario plain the land appears to have been furrowed on a vast scale, with hilly farmland descending toward each of the Finger Lakes only to rise again before the next. The aptly named elongated lakes extend roughly north and south across an 80-mile swath of the state, offering vistas so reminiscent of parts of Switzerland that it's no wonder the city at the northern end of Seneca Lake was named Geneva.

Another distinctly European aspect of the Finger Lakes area is its status as New York State's premier wine-growing region. No longer limited only to the cultivation of native grape varieties, New York's vintners have come a long way, as visits to individual vineyards and the wine museum described below will demonstrate.

Scenes of well-tended vines in rows along steep hillsides may put you in mind of Europe, but the Finger Lakes/Southern Tier region is rich in Americana. Here are museums of coverlets, Victorian dolls, and horse-drawn carriages. You'll even find Mark Twain's study and a museum devoted to Memorial Day.

We'll approach this area from the south, beginning near the Pennsylvania border and continuing up toward Rochester, then heading east along the New York State Thruway and the northern Finger Lakes.

In the city of Elmira there is a site with significant associations in the life of Mark Twain, but one that many Americans—including Twain aficionados familiar with his haunts in Hannibal, Missouri, and Hartford, Connecticut—know little about. This is the **Mark Twain Study,** a charming little summer house on the campus of Elmira College.

Mark Twain married an Elmira woman named Olivia Langdon in 1870, and for many years the author and his family took leave of their palatial Hartford home to spend summers outside Elmira with Olivia's sister, Mrs. Theodore Crane. Mrs. Crane and her husband lived on a farm, where in 1874 they built Twain a freestanding octagonal study, with windows on all sides and a massive stone fireplace. Here Twain wrote *Tom Sawyer* and completed sections of *Huckleberry Finn, Life on the Mississippi, A Connecticut Yankee in King Arthur's Court,* and other works. It was, he said, "the loveliest study you ever saw."

Twain spent his last summer in Elmira in 1903 and returned the following year for his wife's funeral. The author himself was buried in Woodlawn Cemetery, on Walnut Street in Elmira, in 1910.

Having proved difficult to maintain and protect from vandalism, the study was donated to Elmira College by the Langdon family in 1952, whereupon it was removed to its present site on the campus. A Mark Twain exhibit, in nearby Hamilton Hall, includes a typewriter identical to the one Twain once used, a manuscript trunk with the name *Clemens* carved in its lid, and a collection of photographs and some memorabilia relevant to Twain's summer home in Elmira.

The Mark Twain Study, on the Elmira College Campus off Main Street, Elmira, NY 14901, is open during the summer months on Monday through Saturday, 10:00 A.M. to 5:00 P.M., and Sunday, noon to 5:00 P.M. To arrange off-season visits contact The Center for Mark Twain Studies, Quarry Farm, Box 900, Elmira College, Elmira, NY 14901, or call (607) 732–0993.

When Mark Twain's study was at its original site on the Quarry Farm belonging to his in-laws, it commanded a lovely view of the undulating hills along the Chemung River Valley. Little did Twain suspect that within a few decades after his death, these same hills would attract recreationists not content merely to walk the trails and pastures but who would instead soar quietly far above them. By the 1930s Harris Hill, outside Elmira, had become the "Soaring Capital of the United States." The sport of nonmotorized flight is today kept vigorously alive at the **National Soaring Museum,** which offers visitors earthbound exhibits *and* the opportunity to go aloft in sailplanes piloted by experienced professionals from the Harris Hill Soaring Corp.

Regardless of whether you agree with the museum's philosophy that soaring is "flying as nature intended," a visit to the facility offers a good introduction to this often-overlooked aspect of modern aviation. The museum houses the world's largest exhibit of contemporary and historic sailplanes, along with displays explaining the development of soaring and its relation to the parallel fields of meteorology and aerodynamics. You can even climb into a cockpit simulator, similar to those used to teach soaring, and learn what the experience of controlling a motorless plane is like.

Well, almost. To really understand soaring, you have to get off the ground. This can easily be arranged at the museum, or at the Harris Hill Soaring Corp. Visitors' Center, which has a staff of competent pilots, licensed by the Federal Aviation Administration. Just check in at the Harris Hill Gliderport—the rides are available all summer long and on weekends throughout the year, weather permitting. Even if you don't go up yourself, it's fun to watch the graceful, silent flight and landings of the sleek sailplanes.

The National Soaring Museum, Harris Hill, RD #3, Elmira, New York 14903, (607) 734–3128 (office) or 734–0641 (glider field), is open daily, 10:00 A.M. to 5:00 P.M. Call regarding schedules and cost of sailplane flights. To reach the National Soaring Museum, take New York Route 17 to Exit 51 and follow the signs for Harris Hill Park.

Upstream along the Chemung River is Corning, indelibly associated in most travelers' awareness with the Corning Glass Company and its Corning Glass Center and Museum. But there is a worthy newcomer on the Corning Museum scene, **The Rockwell Museum.**

The Rockwell is that rarity among museums, an institution that owes its existence almost entirely to a single individual whose collection it comprises. Robert F. Rockwell is an area native and proprietor of a small department store chain whose interest in Western art dates to his youth spent on a Colorado ranch. He began collecting seriously in the late 1950s, over the years acquiring works not only by universally recognized masters of "cowboy" art such as Charles M. Russell and Frederic Remington but landscapists of the caliber of Albert Bierstadt and Thomas Hill, and animal artists A. F. Tait and Carl Rungius.

Rockwell's protean interests went beyond Western art and sculpture to include an area dear to him as a Corning resident— the beautiful art glass created by Frederick Carder, cofounder of the Steuben Glass Works, which was later incorporated into Corning Glass. Rockwell even collected antique toys, particularly cast iron and mechanical playthings.

By the beginning of the 1980s, Rockwell's collections, particularly of Western art and Carder Steuben glass, were too extensive to be casually shown in his department stores and as part of exhibitions loaned to other institutions. He needed a museum, and one arrived in the form of Corning's old city hall, a Romanesque Revival structure dating from 1893. The Corning Company acquired the building from the city for $1, renovations were undertaken, and in 1982 The Rockwell Museum opened. At present it houses the largest collection of Western art east of the Mississippi, more than two thousand pieces of Carder Steuben glass, Navajo weavings, antique firearms, Indian artifacts, and the toy collection as well.

The Rockwell Museum, Cedar Street, at Denison Parkway

(Route 17), Corning, NY 14830, (607) 937–5386, is open September through June, Monday through Saturday, 9:00 A.M. to 5:00 P.M.; Sunday, noon to 5:00 P.M. During July and August the hours are Monday through Friday, 9:00 A.M. to 7:00 P.M.; Saturday 9:00 A.M. to 5:00 P.M.; Sunday, noon to 5:00 P.M. The museum is closed Thanksgiving, Christmas Eve, Christmas Day, and New Year's Day. There is an admission fee. The Museum Shop, on the premises, sells cards, books, posters, Southwestern jewelry, weavings, baskets, and pottery.

The southern Finger Lakes region is a tranquil, easy-paced corner of the world that nevertheless nurtured one of twentieth-century America's great speed demons. At Hammondsport, on the southern tip of Keuka Lake, the **Glenn H. Curtiss Museum of Local History** chronicles the life works of this native son, who was also a serious pioneer in motorcycling and aviation.

Glenn Hammond Curtiss started out, as did the Wright Brothers, in the bicycle business. He quickly turned to motorcycles, building a V-8-powered bike on which he went over 136 miles per hour in 1907. He also built engines that powered lighter-than-air craft, and in that same year he became involved with Dr. Alexander Graham Bell and other enthusiasts in the "Aerial Experiment Association." Curtiss's engineering helped lift the Association's aeroplane *Red Wing* off the ice of Keuka Lake on the first public flight (as opposed to the Wrights' secret 1903 experiment) of a heavier-than-air craft in the United States.

Glenn Curtiss's accomplishments over the next twenty years dominated the adolescence of aeronautics. In 1910 he landed a plane on water for the first time, and in 1911 he became the first American to receive a pilot's license. In 1919 a Curtiss "flying boat" made the first transatlantic crossing by air. Meanwhile, he had built his Curtiss Aeroplane and Motor Company into an industrial giant employing 10,000 men at the peak of production during World War I. Sensing the traveling trends of the motor age, he even manufactured the first successful house trailers.

The Glenn H. Curtiss Museum of Local History, founded in 1960, houses seven historic aircraft and two reproductions, one of the latter of which is a flyable replica of the inventor's 1908 *June Bug II*. Aviation exhibits also include engines dating from before World War I to 1963, early flight clothing, and instruments. An exhibit devoted to Curtiss's involvement with motorcycling has as its star attraction the V-8 behemoth he rode to his 136.36 mph record in 1907. Non-Curtiss-related items of local historic interest are also on display.

The Glenn H. Curtiss Museum of Local History, Corner of Lake and Main Streets, Hammondsport, NY 14840, (607) 569–2160, is open April 15 through October 31, Monday through Saturday, 9:00 A.M. to 5:00 P.M.; Sundays also from July through October. Admission is $3 for adults; $2.50 for senior citizens; $2 for students; and $1 for children 7–12.

The Finger Lakes region is New York's wine country, and the area around Keuka Lake is in many ways its heart. It was along the shores of Keuka Lake that the late Dr. Konstantin Frank established his Vinifera Vineyards and proved to the world that the European vinifera grapes could survive New York State winters when grafted to hardy American rootstocks. Keuka Lake is also the home of Bully Hill Vineyards, owned by a man who calls himself Walter S. _____. Why? It's a long story, involving the purchase of the Taylor Wine Company by the Coca-Cola Company a few years back (at that time, Mr. _____ was no longer associated with Taylor) and Coke's successful legal action barring the Taylor name from appearing on any labels or promotional literature connected with the products of Mr. _____'s Bully Hill. Can you guess his name now?

In any event, Walter S. _____ is the proprietor not only of Bully Hill but of the **Wine and Grape Museum of Greyton H. Taylor,** G. H. having been none other than his father. (Oops, now we gave it away.) The Museum recounts the story of a century and a half of wine making in New York State, particularly in the Finger Lakes area. It is a museum with a bias, given its proprietor's strong opinions regarding such practices as the mixing of additives into wine or the blending of what he calls "tank car wine" from other states or countries into what is labeled a New York State product. Bully Hill will have none of that sort of thing, and more power to them.

The Wine and Grape Museum of Greyton H. Taylor, G. H. Taylor Memorial Drive, Hammondsport, NY 14840, (607) 868–4814, is open from May 1 through October 31, Monday through Saturday, 10:00 A.M. to 4:30 P.M.; Sunday, noon to 4:30 P.M. There is a museum-affiliated bed-and-breakfast, (607) 868–3226, next door, open May 1 to October 31, and also a moderately priced restaurant. The restaurant specialties include homemade pasta and dishes prepared with wine. The Bully Hill winery may also be visited for tours and tastings; call (607) 868–3210.

Heading northwest away from the Finger Lakes toward the Lake Ontario lowlands, we find the **Genesee Country Village**,

Richard Greeve's *Kiowa*
Genesee Country Village and Museum

and Museum in Mumford, on the southern outskirts of the Rochester area. "Spend a day in the nineteenth century," reads the Museum's invitation—but what's different about this reconstructed village is that they mean the *whole* nineteenth century, not just a small part of it. The fifty-plus buildings originally standing or relocated on this site—all of them restored—represent virtually every stage of the development of upstate New York, from frontier days to late Victorian times.

The rail-fenced pioneer settlement reveals what rural living was like up near Lake Ontario around 1800. Just twenty-five years later the region had prospered to the extent that sumptuous Greek Revival homes such as Livingston Manor, also on the Village grounds, could reflect the rapidly cultivated tastes of the upstate gentry. Turn the pages of another half century, and you find the Victorian quirks and fussy comforts of the 1870 Octagon House, with its tidy cupola and broad verandas. Other Village buildings include a carriage barn, containing a collection of forty horse-drawn vehicles; a Gallery of Sporting Art showcasing paintings and sculpture inspired by wildlife and the hunt; and the George Eastman birthplace, moved here in homage to the man who made nearby Rochester a "film capital" of an entirely different sort than Hollywood, California.

The Genesee Country Village and Museum, off Route 36 in Mumford, NY (mailing address P. O. Box 1819, Rochester, NY 14603), (716) 538–6822, is open from mid-May through mid-October. July and August, open daily, 10:00 A.M. to 5:00 P.M.; spring and fall, open daily, 10:00 A.M. to 4:00 P.M. except Mondays. Admission is $8.50 for adults; $7.50 for senior citizens on weekdays; $5.50 for youth 13–17; $4.00 for children 6–12; children 5 and under are free.

If you picture a little girl in crinoline playing in the parlor of the Country Village's Octagon House, you can well imagine the sort of dolls she might have for companions. Up near Rochester in North Chili, Linda Greenfield has assembled a wonderful collection of these delicate and elaborately dressed playthings in her **Victorian Doll Museum.** The hundreds of dolls at the museum not only reflect the tastes of the Victorian era but also show many types of doll construction that have faded from the picture in these days of molded plastic doll faces and bodies. Here are rudimentary wooden dolls, as well as elaborate dolls made of china, ivory, bisque, and wax. There are even Kewpie dolls—as well as dolls made in the image of famous people, both real and fictional (if you've ever had to buy a Rambo or Brooke Shields doll, you'll understand this phenomenon).

The Victorian Doll Museum premises are also the home of the Chili Doll Hospital, also run by Linda Greenfield. Linda is an expert at doll restoration and repair; her talents extend to mending of heads and limbs, replacement of cloth torsos, leather body repair, and restringing. Dolls are appraised by appointment, and a collector's gift shop offers fine modern and period reproduction specimens.

The Victorian Doll Museum and Chili Doll Hospital, 4332 Buffalo Road, North Chili, NY 14514, (716) 247–0130, is open Tuesday through Saturday, 10:00 A.M. to 4:30 P.M.; Sunday, 1:00 to 4:30 P.M. Admission to the Museum is $1.50 for adults; $.75 for children.

There are dolls and a whole lot more at Rochester's **Margaret Woodbury Strong Museum.** This remarkable institution, the legacy of one woman's interests and devotion to collecting, takes as its theme not only the artifacts of childhood but of all of American life during the decades of our national expansion and industrialization.

Margaret Woodbury Strong (1897–1969) came from a family that owned a buggy whip company. It was, in fact, one of the largest buggy whip concerns in the United States, a fact that might not necessarily have lead to twentieth-century prosperity had not the proceeds been invested wisely. This Margaret's father did, buying stock in a new venture being started by a young Rochester bank clerk named George Eastman, who had a notion that the fun of photography might be spread among the masses. At the time of her death, Margaret Woodbury Strong was the largest individual stockholder in the Eastman Kodak Corporation, and the bequest with which she endowed her museum amounted to $60 million.

With that kind of money, Margaret Woodbury Strong could have acquired only the finest seventeenth-century Dutch masters or dabbled exclusively in Titians and Tintorettos. But she had picked up a far more peripatetic habit of collecting while still a small girl and devoted her career as a grand-scale acquisitor—largely compacted into the last decade of her life—to the purchase of things that instead reflected the preferences of ordinary citizens. Essentially, the collections that form the core of today's Strong Museum reflect middle-class taste from 1820 to 1940, roughly the period in which the old handcrafts and individual modes of expression in utilitarian objects were replaced by the products of the age of industrialization.

The Strong collections, housed since 1982 in an expansive new museum in downtown Rochester, offer a virtual one-stop education in the development of American taste over a century and a quarter of rapid economic growth and social adjustment. Here is one of the largest and best collections of Victorian furniture in the United States, along with a vast sampling of decorative objects—glass, silver, ceramics, and Oriental objects of vertu. There are lithographs, engravings (including much of Winslow Homer's magazine work), rare books, early bicycles, and dollhouses, along with eighty miniature rooms. The sampling of antique dolls is drawn from the 30,000 that Mrs. Strong owned at the time of her death. Other aspects of the collection include mechanical toys, paper ephemera, and costumes.

The Strong Museum has organized its treasures into five major exhibits in the main gallery: "A Century of Childhood, 1820–1920"; "The Face in the Looking Glass: Men, Women, Beauty, and Style, 1820–1940"; "Changing Patterns: Household Furnishings, 1820–1939"; "The Great Transformation" (from rural to urban America in the nineteenth century); and "Gardening in America, 1830–1910." One of the museum's most popular exhibits is an interactive learning/play area designed especially for children. Called "One History Place," it features original and reproduction artifacts from the turn of the century, arranged in kitchen, parlor, and attic settings that allow the children to imagine life in the time of their parents and grandparents. The children can also pretend to travel on a child-size train engine.

The Margaret Woodbury Strong Museum, One Manhattan Square, Rochester, NY 14607, (716) 263–2700, is open Monday through Saturday, 10:00 A.M. to 5:00 P.M.; Sunday, 1:00 to 5:00 P.M.; closed Thanksgiving, Christmas, and New Year's Day. Admission is $2 for adults; $1.50 for senior citizens and students with school ID; and $.75 for children 4–16.

South and east of Rochester is a monument to another important development in the history of American popular culture, the shopping mall. No, this isn't a steel-and-glass mall of the 1950s but a sturdy wooden structure erected in 1879. It was built by Levi Valentine as an all-purpose market and community center for the settlement he was developing, and thus it lays claim to being the first multistore "shopping center" in the United States. Today it houses the **Valentown Museum,** a collection of nineteenth-century small-town memorabilia that includes a re-construction of the first railroad station in the Rochester area and a "Scientific Exhibition," which traveled around the country in a covered wagon from 1825 to 1880.

Valentown Hall, as Valentine called his "mall," had front doors opening into a general store, meat market, cobbler shop, barber shop, bakery, and harness shop. Upstairs were a grange lodge, rooms where classes in the arts and trades were held, and a community ballroom. The ambitious scheme lasted only thirty years, since the promised railroad connection never materialized (the restored station interior belonged to an earlier rail opera-tion). The building was saved from demolition and restored in 1940 by J. Sheldon Fisher, a member of the Fisher family, which gave its name to the present community of Fishers, in which the hall is located. For information on when the Museum may be visited, contact Mr. Fisher at the Valentown Museum, Fishers, NY 14453, (167) 924–2645.

Along with shopping malls, what could be more intrinsic to American civilization than the electronic media? The early days of our fascination with the vacuum tube (a device, young readers, that brought us our news, sports, and "top 40" before the inven-tion of the transitor) are chronicled in the Antique Wireless Asso-ciation's **Electronic Communications Museum** south of the Thruway in East Bloomfield. The museum's collections, housed in the handsome 140-year-old quarters of the East Bloomfield His-torical Society, have been amassed by AWA members throughout the world. They include nineteenth-century telephones (in work-ing order!), some of Marconi's original wireless apparatus, early shipboard wireless equipment, and the crystal radio sets that brought the first broadcast programs into American living rooms. A special attraction is a fully stocked replica of a circa-1925 radio store; another is wireless station W2AN, an actual broadcast op-eration staffed by AWA members. The Museum is sure to fasci-nate anyone who remembers huddling around the old Atwater-Kent for "Gangbusters" and even holds interest for post-war types who can learn how their indispensable televisions were invented. Most amazing of all, the stuff here was actually made in the United States, before the consumer electronics in-dustry migrated to other shores.

The AWA Electronic Communications Museum, just off Routes 5 and 20 in East Bloomfield, NY 14443, (716) 657–7489, is open May 1 to October 31, Sunday, 2:00 to 5:00 P.M.; also open Saturday, 2:00 to 4:00 P.M., and Wednesday, 7:00 to 9:00 P.M., during June, July, and August.

Preserved Americana seems to be the order of the day in this part of upstate New York, and the theme is carried along nicely at the **Granger Homestead and Carriage Museum** in Canandaigua. "Homestead" is actually a bit too homespun a term for this grand Federal mansion, which must have been the talk of Canandaigua and all the farms around when it was built in 1816 by Gideon Granger, a lawyer who had served as postmaster general under Jefferson and Madison. Granger came here to spend the life of a country squire in his retirement, and his descendants lived here until 1930, when they willed many of the furnishings to Rochester's Memorial Art Gallery. The furnishings have been returned to the house on loan since it reopened in 1948. Nine restored rooms contain the furniture of the nineteenth century, including Federal, Empire, and Victorian styles. Decorative objects, original artworks, and China Trade porcelain are also displayed in the rooms. The Homestead houses a gift shop and a new exhibit gallery that focuses on the history of the mansion.

A distinctive attraction of the Granger Homestead is the Carriage Museum, which exhibits more than fifty horse-drawn vehicles made or used in western New York, ranging from coaches and sleighs to delivery wagons and hand-pumped fire-fighting equipment. The sociological implications of the various conveyances on display are explained in an informative exhibit titled "Sleighs and Surreys and Signs and Symbols." As you might suspect, the vehicles used in the days of horsepower said as much about their owners as do the automobiles of our own day.

The Granger Homestead and Carriage Museum, 295 North Main Street, Canandaigua, NY 14424, (716) 394–1472, is open May through October; guided tours are offered on the hour Tuesday through Saturday, 10:00 A.M. to 5:00 P.M., and Sunday, 1:00 to 5:00 P.M. in June, July, and August. Admission is $2.50 for adults and $1 for children. Inquire also about combination admission to the Homestead and Sonnenberg Gardens.

Sonnenberg Gardens are part of an estate built around a mansion representative of a much bolder and expressive architectural aesthetic than Granger's Federal style—this is a Gilded-Age extravaganza, part Tudor Revival, part Queen Anne, built in 1887 by Frederick Ferris Thompson, who founded the First National Bank of the City of New York. The forty-room mansion has been beautifully restored and is well worth a tour—but even more

Japanese Hill Garden with Tea House

impressive than the heavily carved Victorian furniture and fine Oriental rugs contained beneath the house's multicolor slate roof are the gardens themselves.

Frederick Thompson died in 1899, and in 1902 his widow, Mary Clark Thompson, began the extensive formal and informal plantings on the estate as a memorial to her husband. She worked at creating the gardens for the next fourteen years and held occasional "public days" so that her Canandaigua neighbors (she had spent her youth in the town) could enjoy them as well. Since 1973 the gardens have been undergoing restoration, and they appear today much as they did during the first decades of the century.

What sets Sonnenberg Gardens apart is their sheer eclecticism. While many estates of the turn-of-the-century period were planted in a single style, usually formal French or the more naturalistic

English, the gardens here represent just about every major mode of horticultural expression. There is a Japanese Garden, laid out in precise accordance with ancient tradition; an Italian Garden; a sunken parterre display in a Versailles-inspired fleur-de-lis motif; a Colonial Garden reminiscent of the early American plantings of Mt. Vernon and Williamsburg; a garden planted entirely in blue and white flowers; and a Rose Garden containing more than four thousand magnificent bushes blossoming in red, white, and pink. There are also a rock garden, a partially restored Roman bath, a thirteen-house greenhouse complex with a domed palm house conservatory, and fountains and statuary everywhere. After a while, the mansion itself almost seems like an afterthought.

Sonnenberg Gardens, off Route 21N, Canandaigua, NY 14424, (716) 924–5420, is open daily, mid-May through mid-October, 9:30 A.M. to 5:30 P.M. Admission is $5 for adults; $4 for seniors; and $2 for children 6–16.

In the rolling farm country east of Rochester, there is a drumlin—a round, glacially deposited hill—called Cumorah. According to the members of the Church of Jesus Christ of Latter Day Saints, it was on **Hill Cumorah** in September of 1823 that an eighteen-year-old farmboy was told of the existence of a golden book of revelations, buried on the hill fourteen centuries earlier. The boy's name was Joseph Smith, and he said that the messenger who told him about the book was the angel Moroni.

So began the Mormon faith. Or, according to the church's doctrines, so resumed the ministry of Jesus Christ in the New World, because the revelations contained in the Book of Mormon tell of a vanished civilization in upstate New York, among whom Christ preached after his time on earth in Palestine. The golden leaves of the book were purportedly buried by Moroni—then a mortal—after an apocalyptic battle had taken place around Hill Cumorah in the year A.D. 421.

The modern part of the Mormon story continues with Joseph Smith's annual meetings with the angel on Hill Cumorah, the culmination of which, according to Smith, was Moroni's directing him to unearth the scriptures in 1827. Smith told how he translated the book from its unknown ancient language into English, following which—whatever the disputations regarding the work's provenance between Mormons and nonbelievers—he had it published at the print shop of E. B. Grandin in nearby Palmyra. The church itself was organized in Fayette, Seneca County, on April 6, 1830, after which began the westward migrations of the faithful which led to the Mormon-built city of Nauvoo, Illinois, and, after Joseph Smith's assassination and the ascendancy of Brigham Young, to Salt Lake City.

It is interesting to note that Joseph Smith originally came from Vermont, as did Brigham Young and a number of the other early Mormons. After their epiphany and the crystallization of their movement in New York State, they headed west—yet another example of the role this state played as staging area, a transitional place in the expansion of America from its old New England confines to the wide continent beyond.

But back to Hill Cumorah. Though seated now in its world-famous capital of Salt Lake City, the Church of Jesus Christ of Latter Day Saints maintains a strong presence in Palmyra in the form of a large visitor center at Hill Cumorah and an imposing statue of the angel Moroni atop the hill. The visitor center features exhibits, paintings, dioramas, and films explaining Mormon history and beliefs, and the site is the focus each summer (late July) of the "Hill Cumorah Pageant," an elaborately staged sound-and-light drama with a cast of 600, illustrating the ancient and latter-day events relating to the church's founding.

Other historical sites maintained by the LDS church in and around Palmyra include the Joseph Smith home in Manchester; the "Sacred Grove" where he received his first visitation; the printing shop where the Book of Mormon was first published; and the Peter Whitmer farm near Waterloo, where the church was organized. For information on the schedules and locations of each of these sites, as well as on Hill Cumorah itself and the annual pageant, contact the Hill Cumorah Visitors Center, Palmyra, NY 14522, (315) 597-5851.

Palmyra is not without its secular points of interest, one of the most unusual of which is the **Alling Coverlet Museum,** part of the Historic Palmyra Museum located in the village's downtown business district. One never knows where the nation's largest collection of this or that is going to turn up, but when it comes to coverlets the answer is Palmyra.

The bed coverings displayed here were collected over thirty years by Mrs. Merle Alling of Rochester. Heirlooms all, they represent both the simple spreads hand-loomed by farmwives and the somewhat more sophisticated designs woven on multiple-harness looms by professionals during the nineteenth century. Materials include wool, cotton, and linen; the wool and flax (the raw material of linen) were often raised on the same farms whose bedsteads these wonderful examples of folk art once graced. Most owe their rich colors to vegetable dyes, also produced locally. The collection also includes a number of handmade nineteenth-century quilts and several pieces of antique spinning equipment.

A gift shop on the museum's premises offers books on textiles, antique shuttles and bobbins, and local handcrafts.

The Alling Coverlet Museum (Historic Palmyra, Inc.), 122 William Street, Palmyra, NY 14522, (315) 597–6981, is open June through mid-September, daily, 1:00 to 4:00 P.M.; also by appointment. Admission is free, although donations are welcome. Another facet of Historic Palmyra is the **William Phelps General Store Museum.** Erected 1826–28, this commercial building was purchased by William Phelps in 1868 and remained in his family until 1977. Having remained virtually unchanged over the past 120 years, the store, along with its stock, furnishings, and business records, amounts to a virtual time capsule of nineteenth- and early twentieth-century Palmyra. An unusual note: The gas light fixtures in the store and upstairs residential quarters were used by a Phelps family member until 1976, electricity never having been installed in the building.

The William Phelps General Store Museum, 140 Market Street, Palmyra, NY 14522, (315) 597–6981, is open June through September, Saturday, 1:00 to 4:00 P.M. Admission is free.

From coverlets to clocks . . . the northern Finger Lakes region seems to be New York State's attic, filled with interesting collections of things we might otherwise take for granted. In Newark, the **Hoffman Clock Museum** comprises more than a hundred clocks and watches collected by local jeweler and watchmaker Augustus L. Hoffman. Housed in a separate section of the Newark Public Library, the collection includes timepieces from Great Britain, Europe, and Japan, although the majority of the clocks and watches are of nineteenth-century American manufacture with more than a dozen having been made in New York State. Each summer, the Museum's curator mounts a special exhibit devoted to a particular aspect of the horologist's art.

The Hoffman Clock Museum, Newark Public Library, 121 High Street, Newark, NY 14513, (315) 331–4370, is open weekdays, 9:30 A.M. to 9:00 P.M.; Saturday (except during July and August), 9:30 A.M. to 5:30 P.M.. Admission is free.

Waterloo, New York, is the birthplace of Memorial Day and the home of the **Memorial Day Museum.** It was in the village of

Waterloo, in the summer of 1865, that a patriotic businessman named Henry C. Welles put forward the idea of honoring the soldiers who fell in the Civil War by placing flowers on their graves on a specified day of observance. Such an idea no doubt surfaced in many towns and cities across the republic in the aftermath of the War Between the States, but Waterloo actually did something about it. On May 5 of the following year, thanks to the efforts of Welles and Civil War veteran Gen. John B. Murray, the village was draped in mourning, and a contingent of veterans and townspeople marched to the local cemeteries and with appropriate ceremonies decorated their comrades' graves. The tradition which thus began soon spread to other communities, and within two years the date of observance had been standardized as May 30. This, of course, all took place before the thirst for three-day weekends led to the concept of the movable secular feast.

In 1966 President Johnson signed a proclamation officially naming Waterloo the birthplace of Memorial Day. On May 29 of that same Memorial Day centennial year, Waterloo's new Memorial Day Museum was opened in a reclaimed mansion in the heart of town. The twenty-room, once-derelict brick structure is itself a local treasure, especially distinguished by the ornate ironwork on its veranda. Although built in the early Italianate Revival era of 1836–50, the house is being restored to its appearance circa 1860–70—the decade of the Civil War and the first Memorial Day observances.

The Museum's collections concentrate upon the Civil War, as well as the lives and era of the originators of the holiday. During its first twenty years of operation, the museum has expanded its holdings to include memorabilia from both World Wars and the Korean conflict.

The Memorial Day Museum, 35 East Main Street, Waterloo, NY 13165, (315) 539–9611, is open from Memorial Day through Labor Day, weekdays except Monday, 1:30 to 4:00 P.M. Admission is free, although donations are welcome.

Some institutions, such as the Memorial Day Museum, have a pinpoint focus; others follow a more eclectic pattern of acquisition and education. Occasionally, a small institution finds its focus as it matures, as is the case with the **Cayuga Museum** in Auburn. Founded in 1936 and devoted to exhibiting important small collections of objects as diverse as Oriental rugs, North American and South American Indian art, dolls, and art from the Philippines, the Cayuga Museum has in recent years turned its attention to the lifework of one of Auburn's most illustrious citi-zens, Theodore W. Case. Case was the man who figured out how to record sound and images simultaneously, thus making possi-ble the motion picture soundtrack. Much of his work was done with Earl Sponable at the Case Research Laboratory, which is now in the process of restoration as the Museum's Case-Sponable Hall of Light and Sound.

Partially implemented plans for the Case-Sponable facility include display of the inventors' cameras, projectors, and recording equip-ment; a hands-on exhibit area featuring explanations of sound film-making techniques; and an auditorium for the showing of historic silent and sound films. Of course, the museum continues to exhibit its art and historical collections, grouped into sections representing early Americana (pioneer-era tools and household utensils), indige-nous American art, and upstate New York Victoriana. There is also a replica of the log-cabin birthplace of president Millard Fillmore, who was born just south of here in Genoa.

The Cayuga Museum, 203 Genesee Street, Auburn, NY 13021, (315) 253–8051, is open Monday through Friday, 1:00 to 5:00 P.M.; Saturday, 10:00 A.M. to noon and 1:00 to 5:00 P.M.; Sunday, 2:00 to 5:00 P.M. Admission is free.

We haven't had too much to say in these pages on the subject of restaurants, and that has been a deliberate decision: If we stopped for a bite in every town along the way, there would be no room for Victorian dolls or Millard Fillmore's birthplace. But in the town of Skaneateles, on the Finger Lake of the same name, there is a restau-rant that serves as a living museum of a certain style of American eating, back before obsessive slenderness became a national preoc-cupation. This is **The Krebs,** a place where it is always Sunday afternoon and your grandmother is always fixing dinner.

The Krebs began back in 1899, when Mr. and Mrs. Fred Krebs first opened their doors to a local clientele. Since then, the menu has remained fixed upon the dining preferences of 1899 small-town America. As for the setting, think "parlor" instead of "living room" and you'll be on the right track. The nouvelle-minimalist approach is no more in evidence here in the furnishings than it is on the plates.

Dinner at the Krebs (aside from Sunday brunch, dinner is the only meal served) is always table d'hote, with a minimum of choices. You can choose from among simple starter courses such as shrimp cocktail, fruit cup, and (not *or*) clear or cream soups, but then the serious, standard menu kicks in: lobster newburg, followed by half a broiled chicken and roast beef. Accompaniments include homemade breads, rolls, and relishes, candied sweet potato, fresh vegetables, creamed mushrooms. . .all good, honest Sunday dinner fare. Then they bring out the homemade pies, and brownies, and cake.

Of course we like mousseline of pheasant and crispy Szechuan fish. But every now and then, it's nice to get back to the old-time kitchen religion—sort of like turning off Vivaldi and putting on the ball game. And here you have it, at the Krebs.

The Krebs, 53 West Genesee Street (Route 20), Skaneateles, NY 13152, (315) 685–5714 or 685–7001, is open from early May through late October. They serve dinner from 6:00 until 9:00 P.M. Monday through Thursday; Friday and Saturday dinner from 6:00 to 10:00 P.M.; Sunday brunch from 10:30 A.M. to 2:00 P.M.; and Sunday dinner from 4:00 to 9:00 P.M. Reservations are strongly recommended, and credit cards are accepted.

Now what you need is a walk—preferably to Nebraska, if you want to work off every last calorie, although a day at the **Beaver Lake Nature Center** in Baldwinsville will do. The center is an Onandaga County Park incorporating several different ecosystems, all connected by 9 miles of well-maintained hiking trails. Among the plant communities are a bog (accessible by boardwalk), upland meadows and hardwood forests, a cattail marsh, and conifer stands. A 200-acre lake, offering beautiful vistas but no recreational facilities, is a migration-time magnet for up to 30,000 Canada geese. Guided canoe tours of the lake are available during the summer; rental canoes are available for these tours, and you must preregister. The entire center is a great place for birders; more than 180 species have been sighted here over the years.

The informative Beaver Lake Visitor Center is the starting point for a regular schedule of hour-long guided tours of the trails given by professional naturalists each weekend in winter. The marked trails are ideal for snowshoeing or cross-country skiing. Wildflowers are abundant in springtime, and the hardwoods put on their annual show of color in September and October.

Beaver Lake Nature Center, 8477 East Mud Lake Road, Baldwinsville, NY 13027, (315) 638–2519, is open all year, daily, dawn to dusk. Admission is free. Call ahead to register for guided nature tours. There is a nature-oriented gift shop in the Visitor Center.

Off the Beaten Path along the Lakeshore

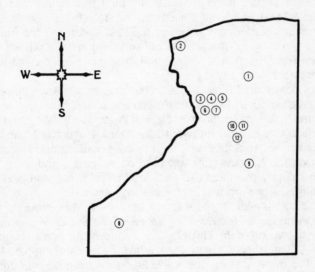

1. Oak Orchard and Tonawanda Wildlife Management Areas
2. Old Fort Niagara
3. Allentown
4. Theodore Roosevelt Inaugural Site
5. Frank Lloyd Wright Houses
6. Q-R-S Music Rolls
7. Buffalo Museum of Science
8. Chautauqua Institution
9. Arcade and Attica Railroad
10. Roycroft Campus
11. Elbert Hubbard Museum
12. Millard Fillmore House

The Lakeshore

Ever since the Erie Canal was opened a century and a half ago, New York City and Buffalo have assumed a front door-back door status in New York State. New York City became the Empire State's gateway to the world, a capital of international shipping and finance. The docksides and railyards of Buffalo, meanwhile, were the portals through which the industrial output and raw materials of the Midwest flowed into the state. Buffalo became an important "border" city between the East Coast and the hinterlands, a center of manufacturing and flour milling whose fortunes have risen and fallen with the state of the nation's smokestack economy.

But don't write Buffalo off as an old lunchbucket town that gets too much snow in the winter. Buffalo has some impressive architecture, from Louis Sullivan's splendid Prudential Building and the art deco City Hall downtown, to the Frank Lloyd Wright houses described below. South Park, with its conservatory, and Riverside Park on the Niagara offer welcome open spaces, and there are even culinary treasures like Buffalo chicken wings and beef on weck (roast beef on a delicate caraway seed roll.)

The countryside at the western tip of New York provides further evidence as to why Niagara Falls isn't the only reason to drive to the end of the Thruway. The Pennsylvania border country boasts giant Allegany State Park, a hiking and camping paradise, and the byways along the Lake Erie shore wander through a picture-pretty territory dotted with vineyards, cherry orchards, and roadside stands selling delicious goat's-milk fudge. Yes, goat's-milk fudge. It's the little serendipities that make traveling fun.

Just to mix things up a bit, we'll venture out into the sticks to begin what is otherwise a chapter with a strong urban emphasis. Only 40 miles northeast of Buffalo is a pristine tract of some 19,000 acres, the core of which (11,000 acres) makes up the federal Iroquois National Wildlife Refuge. On either side of the refuge are the **Oak Orchard** (east) and **Tonawanda** (west) **Wildlife Management Areas,** operated by the state of New York's Department of Environmental Conservation. Both the Oak Orchard and Tonawanda areas are primarily wetlands, with plenty of access trails on high ground, that offer superb opportunities not only for hunters (during designated seasons) but for hikers and birders as well.

Both the 5,600-acre Tonawanda tract and the 2,500-acre Oak Orchard area owe their status as superb waterfowl habitats to human intervention in what was already a natural wetland. The Oak Orchard Swamp, after which the smaller area is named, was the result of a limestone outcrop that substantially blocks the flow of Oak Orchard Creek near the town of Shelby Center, thus creating a vast upstream wetland. Tonawanda (not to be confused with the city near Buffalo) lies just to the southwest, on the Tonawanda Creek floodplain. Before the state took control of these lands, the flooding that made the area so attractive to migrating waterfowl was largely a spring phenomenon. But the building of dikes and other water-level control structures has resulted in the creation of a total of 3,000 acres of permanent marshland, allowing birds to nest here even after late spring and to use the area as a resting stop on their fall migration as well. The management plan even calls for the planting of feed grains to supplement naturally occurring waterfowl forage.

The best time for birders to visit Tonawanda and Oak Orchard is from early March to mid-May. That's when more than 100,000 Canada geese along with lesser numbers of black, pintail, and mallard ducks, American wigeon, teal, and shoveler and ring-necked ducks pause on their northward migration, with some staying to nest. The transitional habitat along the borders of the marsh attracts shore and wading birds and migrating spring warblers.

To learn more about the hiking, canoeing, birding, and hunting opportunities at the Tonawanda and Oak Orchard Wildlife Management Areas, stop in at the Iroquois National Wildlife Refuge headquarters, 1101 Casey Road, Alabama, NY 14003, (716) 948–5445. Open Monday through Friday from 7:30 A.M. to 4:00 P.M., the headquarters provides information on regional wildlife-protection areas and offers interpretive walks on its own trails and films in its auditorium. At the Oak Orchard area, visit the self-guided exhibits at the Oak Orchard Education Center on Knowlesville Road, just north of the town of Oakfield. The Center is open daily from sunrise to sunset and is the starting point for four nature trails. An observation tower is located on Albion Road, also at the Oak Orchard area. For additional information, contact the regional wildlife manager of the New York State Department of Environmental Conservation, 6274 East Avon-Lima Road, Avon NY 14414, (716) 226–2466.

It seems as if it isn't possible to tick off too many miles in this

Drummer—Fort Niagara

state without encountering one of the string of forts that once defended the thirteen colonies' northwestern frontier and played so prominent a role not only in the struggles between the British and French for North American supremacy but in our own war for independence as well. The westernmost of these (in New York, at least) is **Old Fort Niagara,** located in Fort Niagara State Park downstream from Niagara Falls at the point where the Niagara River flows into Lake Ontario.

Fort Niagara occupies what was, in the days of conventional warfare, one of the most strategic locations in all of the interior of North America. The first European to realize that whoever held this spot would control traffic between Lakes Erie and Ontario was Robert Cavalier, Sieur de la Salle, the great French explorer. Here, in 1678, he built Fort Conti, the first of the site's defenses. Abandoned the following year, Fort Conti was followed by Fort Denonville (1687–88) and finally by the great "French Castle" erected here in 1726. The Castle served as the core of Fort Niagara's defenses through nearly a century of intermittent warfare and was in use as officers' housing as recently as World War I. Now restored to its eighteenth-century appearance, it is the focal point of Old Fort Niagara.

The French Castle and its outer defenses fell to the British in 1759, following a nineteen-day siege. A British garrison held the fort throughout the American Revolution, having strengthened its defenses with the addition of the North and South Redoubts, which survive today. It was 1797 before a treaty finally forced Great Britain to cede Fort Niagara to the United States, but the installation was seized again by British troops in 1813. Returned to American control in 1815, it has been peaceful ever since, although it continued as a commissioned fort throughout the period of tensions with Canada in the mid 1800s. Finally relegated to service as a training facility, the fort was closed by the U.S. government in 1963—just fifteen years short of the tercentennial of La Salle's Fort Conti.

Restored between the years of 1927 and 1934, the older buildings of Fort Niagara are maintained by the nonprofit, private Old Fort Niagara Association in cooperation with the state of New York. Visitors may tour not only the refurbished French Castle but the British-built North and South Redoubts, the battery upon which artillery was mounted by the Americans during the War of 1812, and the American land and river defenses of the mid-nineteenth century. Beyond the silent military structures there are broad vistas of Lake Ontario and, in clear weather, the rising mists of Niagara Falls 14 miles to the south.

Old Fort Niagara, Fort Niagara State Park, Youngstown, NY 14174, (716) 745–7611, is open daily, July 1 through Labor Day, 9:00 A.M. to 7:30 P.M.; during the rest of the year, daily opening is at 9:00 A.M., although seasonal closing times vary. Closed Thanksgiving, Christmas, and New Year's Day. During the summer, there are frequent costumed re-enactments of military drills, with musket and cannon firings. Admission is $3 for adults; $2.25 for senior citizens and teenagers; and $.85 for children 6–12.

Heading upriver (or, more likely, down Route I-190) we pass Niagara Falls and come to the terminus town of the Erie Canal, in its day, and the New York State Thruway in ours—Buffalo. For a quick introduction to this sprawling inland port, head downtown to reconnoiter the city and Lake Erie from the twenty-eighth floor observatory of City Hall (open weekdays, from 9:00 A.M. to 3:00

P.M.), and then visit the nearby historic neighborhood of **Allentown.** In 1827, when Lewis Allen bought 29 acres of farmland here, this was just beyond the northern boundaries of the young village of Buffalo. In those days, what is now Allen Street was a path used by the farmer's cows, but the successive development of rural estates, suburban subdivision, and finally full-scale urbanization made Allentown the residential heart of the growing city. In a scenario repeated throughout the northeastern United States, the middle of our century found Allentown run-down and forgotten—but by the 1980s, community activists and rehabilitation specialists, organized as the Allentown Association, had become determined not to let the neighborhood slip into oblivion. The result of their efforts has been the substantial revival of the blocks surrounding Allen Street, east of Main, and the identification of a number of formerly neglected points of interest.

The works of a number of important architects, and the homes of several famous people, are tucked into the compact Allentown neighborhood. Representative of the district's myriad building styles are the Kleinhans Music Hall on Symphony Circle, designed in 1938 by Eliel and Eero Saarinen; the 1869 Dorsheimer Mansion, 434 Delaware Avenue, an early work of the peerless Henry Hobson Richardson; Stanford White's 1899 Butler Mansion (672 Delaware) and 1895 Pratt Mansion (690 Delaware); and a lovely example of the Flemish Renaissance style at 267 North Street. As for the haunts of the famous, there are the childhood home of F. Scott Fitzgerald, 29 Irving Street; the home of artist Charles Burchfield (once a designer for a Buffalo wallpaper company) at 459 Franklin Street; and, at 472 Delaware Avenue, the carriage house belonging to the now-vanished house occupied circa 1870 by the editor and part owner of the *Buffalo Morning Express,* a man who hated Buffalo: Samuel Langhorne Clemens, whom we met back in Elmira under the name of Mark Twain.

One house in the Allentown neigborhood stands above all others in historic importance. For fifty years the home of prominent Buffalo lawyer Ansley Wilcox, the Greek Revival house at 641 Delaware Avenue became part of American legend on September 14, 1901, when a vigorous young man who had just rushed in from a vacation in the Adirondacks stepped into the library to take the oath of office as president of the United States. William McKinley was dead, the victim of an assassin; the era of Theodore Roosevelt was about to begin.

The story of that fateful day and the tragic event that preceded it is told at the **Theodore Roosevelt Inaugural National His-**

toric Site, as the Wilcox house has been known since its restoration and opening to the public in 1971. Perhaps the most interesting aspect of the tale concerns the mad dash Roosevelt made from the Adirondacks to Buffalo. He had gone to the city and stayed for a few days at the Wilcox house after McKinley was shot by an anarchist at the Pan-American Exposition but had left to join his family at their mountain retreat after being assured by the President's doctors that his condition had stabilized. Notified several days later of McKinley's worsening state, the vice-president made an overnight journey by horse and wagon to the nearest train station, where he learned that the president was dead. Roosevelt and his party then raced to Buffalo in a special train. Within two hours after his arrival, he was standing in Wilcox's library, wearing borrowed formal clothes as he took the oath as the nation's twenty-sixth president.

The Theodore Roosevelt Inaugural National Historic Site, 641 Delaware Avenue, Buffalo, NY 14202, (716) 884–0095, is open Monday through Friday, 9:00 A.M. to 5:00 P.M.; weekends, noon to 5:00 P.M. It is closed on Saturdays, January through March. Closed January 1, Memorial Day, July 4, Labor Day, Thanksgiving Day, and Christmas Day. A small admission fee is charged.

The residential neighborhoods north of the downtown and Allentown areas of Buffalo boast five examples of the work of America's greatest architect, **Frank Lloyd Wright.** Wright's residential architecture is generally distributed within the central and upper Midwest, where he brought his "prairie style" to maturity. The fact that there exists a pocket of the master's work in Buffalo is due to his having designed a house in Oak Park, Illinois, for the brother of John D. Larkin, founder of the Larkin Soap Company of Buffalo. Larkin liked his brother's house and brought Wright to Buffalo to design the company headquarters. The Larkin Building, a light, airy masterpiece of commercial architecture, stood on Seneca Street, from 1904 until it was unconscionably demolished in 1950. But fate was kinder to the five Buffalo houses built for Larkin Company executives following Wright's arrival in town, all of which survive to this day. Here is a list of the houses and their locations:

• William Heath House, 76 Soldiers Place, corner of Bird Avenue. Completed in 1906, the Heath House faces the green expanse of Soldiers Place, landscaped by Frederick Law Olmsted. Look for the architect's distinctive geometrically patterned leaded-glass casement windows. (Private; not open to visitors.)

• Darwin D. Martin House, 125 Jewett Parkway, corner of Summit Avenue. Also completed in 1906, this expansive home was unfortunately left vacant for seventeen years prior to the mid '50s, during which time half of the original Wright windows were lost. It was restored in 1970 by the State University of New York at Buffalo, which uses it for offices. For information regarding tours, contact the School of Architecture and Planning, Hayes Hall, (716) 831–3485, 125 Jewett Parkway Buffalo, NY 14214.

• George Barton House, 118 Summit Avenue. Built in 1903–4, the Barton House is a smaller brick structure with distinctive top-story casement windows and a broad roof overhang, built on land adjacent to the estate of Darwin Martin, Mrs. Barton's brother. (Private; not open to visitors.)

•Gardener's Cottage, Martin Estate, 285 Woodward Avenue. Constructed in 1906, the cottage is one of the few surviving service buildings of the Martin estate. Additions to the rear were made in 1948 and 1956. Restoration is under way. (Private; not open to visitors.)

•Walter Davidson House, 57 Tillinghast Place. With the exception of Darwin Martin's 1926 summer house built south of the city on a bluff above Lake Erie, the 1909 Davidson House is the last of Wright's Buffalo residences. It is also the only one of the group with a stucco exterior, which gives it a delicate strength that blends superbly with the site landscaping. (Private; not open to visitors.)

From what we know about Frank Lloyd Wright, we can surmise that if he ever caught a client putting a player piano in one of his houses, he would have rapped him across the knuckles with his walking stick. But the perennially old-fashioned machines began to flourish during the first decade of the twentieth century, when Wright was designing his radically modern houses, and they are with us still. Nowadays, the most complete line of rolls for player pianos is manufactured and sold by a Buffalo institution called **Q-R-S Music Rolls.**

Q-R-S is one of the last (and also the oldest) manufacturers of player-piano rolls in the United States, having been founded in 1900 by Melville Clark, the man who perfected the player. During the heyday of the instrument in the 1920s, Q-R-S had plants in New York, Chicago, and San Francisco, but by 1966 only a small facility in the Bronx remained. A new owner bought the company and moved it to Buffalo, where subsequent ownership has kept it.

A piano-roll company like Q-R-S dosen't stay in business simply by cranking out reprints of "Sweet Adeline" and "You Are My

Sunshine." Instead, the firm's list of offerings is constantly expanding, as specialists at the Buffalo plant arrange recent hits for piano and then transfer the notes to rolls, creating masters for subsequent production runs. Thus you can buy rolls for the song "Don't Worry, Be Happy," the Beach Boys' "Kokomo," and other tunes penned long after your player was built.

But not all player pianos are antiques. The company is making an interface device that will enable a home computer to play music programmed on a floppy disk through an electronic synthesizer.

Whether or not floppy disks are the player-piano rolls of the future, the fact remains that Q-R-S is selling about a half million traditional rolls each year and is constantly adding to its list. You can order a copy of the current catalogue through the mail, but if you're in the area it's a lot more fun to stop in at the factory and make your purchase after taking a tour. Q-R-S Music Rolls, 1026 Niagara Street, Buffalo, NY 14213, (716) 885–4600, is open Monday through Friday 9:00 A.M. to 4:00 P.M., with tours at 10:00 A.M. and 2:00 P.M.

Set against the beautiful landscaping of Martin Luther King, Jr., Park (formerly Humboldt Park) the **Buffalo Museum of Science** fulfills an important regional teaching role in the earth sciences and natural history, with exhibits and interpretive displays devoted to subjects as diverse as dinosaurs, astronomy, American Indians, Egyptian mummies and artifacts, and the processes of evolution. But the museum has made a special effort in the field of insects. Insect exhibit areas are divided along conceptual and geographical lines, the idea being to get as far as possible from the old butterflies-pinned-to-a-board method of explaining the tremendous variety of the insect world. Instead, free use is made of enormously enlarged photographic slides of insect species, arranged according to habitat, and a video presentation tells about the lives and behavior of insects.

Two of the principal exhibit areas in the museum's insect section are concerned with a pair of vastly different ecosystems—the cloud forest in the coastal Andean highlands of north central Venezuela and the Niagara frontier region of New York State, which constitutes the museum's own backyard. A cloud forest is a cool, moist, high-elevation environment, marked by lush vegetation and a rich variety of animal life; the Venezuelan cloud forest of the Rancho Grande biological research station, which provides the focus for the museum's exhibit, hosts not only 1,300 species of birds and a wealth of reptilian and mammalian species, but all known orders of insects.

The Niagara Frontier display area illustrates the biological diversity of Buffalo's home ecosystem, a transitional zone along the Ontario-Erie Basin. Western New York State may not seem as exotic a place as the highlands of Venezuela, but it nevertheless harbors a significant proportion of the state's 16,000-plus insect species. A diorama based upon conditions found on local farmland helps to explain the ecological niches that some of the species occupy.

The Buffalo Museum of Science, Humboldt Parkway, Buffalo, NY 14211, (716) 896–5200, is open daily, 10:00 A.M. to 5:00 P.M. Closed New Year's Day, July 4, Thanksgiving Day, and Christmas Day. Admission is $2.50 for adults; $1 for senior citizens, children 4–17, and students with ID.

The southwestern tip of New York State is the home of a century-old enterprise that exemplifies the American penchant for self-improvement. The **Chautauqua Institution,** on Chautauqua Lake, gave its name to an endless array of itinerant tent-show lyceums around the turn of the century. A lot of us have forgotten, though, that the original institution is still thriving right where it was founded in 1874. Chautauqua's progenitors were Bishop John Heyl Vincent and the industrialist (and father-in-law of Thomas Edison) Lewis Miller, and their original modest goal was the establishment of a school for Sunday school teachers. Chautauqua grew to become a village unto itself, offering not only religious instruction but a program of lectures and adult-education courses.

The largely secularized Chautauqua of today bears little resemblance to the Methodist camp meeting of a hundred years ago, although services in the major faiths are held daily. The character of the place in the 1980s owes at least as much to the founding here of the Chautauqua Literary and Scientific Circle, a turn-of-the-century self-education program based upon the great books of the Western tradition. The Chautauqua emphasis on culture and mental and spiritual improvement has led to an extensive annual summer calendar of lectures, concerts, dramatic performances, and long- and short-term courses in subjects ranging from foreign languages to computers to creative writing. It has its own 30,000-volume library.

For performing-arts enthusiasts there are four professional companies that perform throughout the season: The Chautauqua

Symphony Orchestra, The Chautauqua Conservatory Theater Company, The Chautauqua Dance Festival, and The Chautauqua Opera Company.

To put it simply, Chautauqua is a vast summer camp of self-improvement, a place where you can rock (in chairs) on broad verandas, walk tree-lined streets that have no cars, and listen in on a chamber music rehearsal on your way to lunch. Recreational opportunities include a twenty-seven-hole golf course, tennis, softball, fishing, sailing, waterskiing, wind surfing, boating, canoeing, cycling, boccie ball, shuffleboard, volleyball, and swimming at four beaches.

The season at Chautauqua lasts for nine weeks each summer, but admission is available on a daily, weekend, or weekly basis. Each admission ticket gives its bearer the virtual run of the community and covers virtually all evening amphitheater events, lectures, and artistic performances except operas and plays. For overnight guests, lodging and meals are available at a number of locations on the Chautauqua grounds; accommodations vary from the Victorian elegance of American-plan hotels to modest apartments rented on a seasonal basis.

For complete information on facilities and programs, contact Chautauqua Institution, Chautauqua, NY 14722, (716) 357–6200 or (800) 333–0884.

If you were heading off to a summer at Chautauqua three generations ago, you would of course have gotten there by rail— specifically, by a steam-hauled train of the Erie, Pennsylvania, or New York Central railroads. Of course, Amtrak can get you there today (nearest station: Erie, Pennsylvania), but if you want steam you'll have to head to a nostalgia operation like the **Arcade and Attica Railroad,** headquartered just southeast of Buffalo in Arcade.

Maybe *nostalgia* isn't the right word, since the Arcade and Attica is real working railroad with a healthy freight clientele. But the company's passenger operation is an unabashed throwback, relying for motive power on a pair of circa-1920 coalburners pulling old, open-window steel coaches that once belonged to the Delaware, Lackawanna, and Western.

Actually, the Arcade and Attica's tourist-oriented passenger run is the company's second venture into the business of hauling people as well as freight. In 1951 the firm abandoned its regular passenger operations, having discovered that ticket revenues for the first quarter of that year amounted to all of $1.80! (In those

Acrade and Attica Railroad, Arcade

days the line did indeed connect Arcade and Attica, but service north of North Java was abandoned in 1957 after a washout just south of Attica.) But in 1962 the A&A management decided that if it reinvested in previously abandoned steam power, people might come just to ride the train for fun. They did, and they still do. A&A passengers enjoy a ninety-minute ride through some of upstate's loveliest farm country, ending right where they started by way of a trip back through time.

The Arcade and Attica Railroad, 278 Main Street, Arcade, NY 14009, (716) 496–9877, operates weekends from Memorial Day through the end of October, with Wednesday trips during July and August. Call ahead for schedules. Tickets are available at the 278 Main Street office.

Along with steam engines and the Chautauqua, one of the true institutions of turn-of-the-century America was a self-made philosopher named Elbert Hubbard. In addition to writing a little "preachment" (as he called it) titled "A Message to Garcia" that dealt with the themes of loyalty and hard work, and publishing his views in a periodical called the *Philistine,* Hubbard was famous for having imported the design aesthetic and celebration of handcrafts fostered in England by the artist and poet William Morris. Elbert Hubbard became the chief American proponent of the Arts and Crafts Movement, which touted the virtues of honest craftsmanship in the face of an increasing late-nineteenth-century tendency toward machine production of furniture, printed matter, and decorative and utilitarian household objects. Visually, the style absorbed influences as diverse as art nouveau and American Indian crafts and is familiar to most of us in the form of solid, oaken, slat-sided Morris chairs and the simple "Mission" furniture of Gustav Stickley. Elbert Hubbard not only wrote about such stuff, he set up a community of craftsmen to turn it out—furniture, copper, leather, even printed books. He called his operation The Roycrofters, and it was headquartered on a "campus" in **East Aurora, New York.**

There are several ways the modern traveler can savor the spirit of Elbert Hubbard in modern East Aurora. One is by visiting the **Roycroft Campus,** on South Grove Street. The campus grounds, now a National Historic Site, feature a gift shop, working pottery, art gallery, and several antiques dealers, all housed in Hubbard-era buildings. Just across the street, at 40 South Grove Street, Hubbard's own Roycroft Inn remains closed as of this writing, although the owner, a Rochester foundation dedicated to preserving western New York landmarks, hopes to find a developer who will reopen the Art-and-Crafts-style structure as a public accommodation.

Another window on the Roycroft era is the **Elbert Hubbard Museum,** recently relocated in a circa-1910 bungalow built by Roycroft craftsmen. Part of the furnishings, including the superb Arts-and-Crafts dining room, are original and were the property of centenarian Grace ScheideMantel when she turned the house over to the museum in 1985. (Mrs. ScheideMantel's husband, George, once headed the Roycroft leather department.) Other Roycroft products on display at the house include hammered copperware, bookcases with leaded-glass inserts, oak chapel benches, a magnificent stained-glass lamp by the Roycroft designer Dard Hunter, an oil portrait of Elbert Hubbard, and a saddle custom-made for Hubbard just prior to his death on the torpedoed *Lusitania* in 1915.

The Elbert Hubbard Museum (ScheideMantel House), 363 Oakwood Avenue, East Aurora, NY 14052, (716) 652–4735, is open from June 1 to mid-October on Wednesday, Saturday, and Sunday, 2:00 to 4:00 P.M.; by appointment the rest of the year. A $1 donation is requested. Private or group tours also can be arranged, year-round, by appointment.

Before taking leave of East Aurora, and the Buffalo-Lakeshore region as well, we should stop in at the home of one of our least-appreciated presidents, Millard Fillmore. Fillmore, who was born in the Finger Lakes town of Genoa in 1800, came to East Aurora to work as a lawyer in 1825. He built this house (since moved to its present Shearer Avenue location) on Main Street, in the village, in the same year, and he lived here with his wife until 1830. As restored and furnished by previous owners and the Aurora Historical Society, the cottage contains country furnishings of Fillmore's era, as well as more refined pieces in the Greek Revival or "Empire" style of the president's early years. A high desk to be used while standing was part of the furnishings in Fillmore's law office; the rear parlor, added in 1930, showcases furniture owned by the Fillmores in later years, when they lived in a Buffalo mansion. The large bookcase was used in the White House during the Fillmore presidency.

The **Millard Fillmore House National Landmark** (Aurora Historical Society) 24 Shearer Avenue, East Aurora, NY 14052, (716) 652–3280, is open from June 1 to mid-October, Wednesday, Saturday, and Sunday, 2:00 to 4:00 P.M.; by appointment the rest of the year. Admission is $1 for adults; children free.

Off the Beaten Path in the Catskills

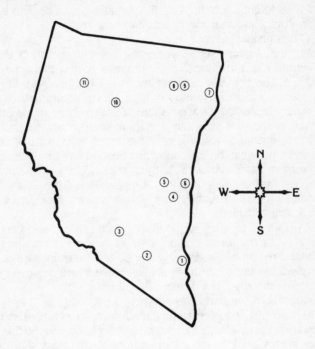

1. Constitution Island
2. Hall of Fame of the Trotter and Trotting Horse Museum
3. Wurtsboro Airport
4. Huguenot Street
5. Delaware and Hudson Canal Museum
6. Slabsides
7. Bronck Museum
8. Durham Center Museum
9. Richter's Butterfly Museum
10. Burroughs Memorial
11. Hanford Mills Museum

The Catskills

To many lifelong New York City residents for whom the Adirondacks might as well be the other side of the moon, the Catskills *are* upstate New York. At this point in our travels, we certainly know better—but nevertheless, if you only had a couple of days to get out of the City, the Catskills would be your best bet for a quick introduction to exurban New York.

The Catskills, of course, are "mountains" in the Eastern rather than the Western sense. Generally lower in elevation than the Adirondacks, these are old, worn peaks, part of the Appalachian Range. The higher elevations are to the north, where the larger ski areas are located. But some of the most dramatic Catskills scenery lies along the west shore of the Hudson, within 30 or 40 miles of the New York City line. Here are the majestic Palisades, brooding cliffs of volcanic basalt exposed by millions of years of water and weather; here also are Bear Mountain, Tallman, and Harriman state parks, with their thick forests and panoramic views. Farther west are the abrupt cliffs of the Shawangunk Mountains, where some of the world's greatest rock climbers perfect their technique.

A place of mystery to the early Dutch settlers, and later a virtual synonym for a certain style of resort entertainment, the Catskill region has a history as varied as its terrain. We'll start our exploration at the south, near the Hudson, and move north and then west toward the farther hills.

Just about everyone knows where West Point is, but how many Hudson Valley travelers or military buffs can locate **Constitution Island?** Geographical literalists might look for it in the first chapter of this book, since it's practically on the east shore of the Hudson, separated from the mainland only by marshes. But since visitors have to take a boat to get to the island, and since the boat leaves from West Point, here we have it among our Catskills sites.

Although Constitution Island never served any military purpose after the Revolutionary War, it had an important part to play in General Washington's strategy for keeping British naval traffic out of the upper Hudson River. During the earlier part of the war the fortifications on the island were relatively ineffectual; begun in 1775, "Fort Constitution" was still unfinished when it was captured by the British under Sir Henry Clinton two years later. Largely destroyed by its American defenders before they retreated, the fort was never rebuilt.

By the following year, however, the island was back in American hands and was more valuable than ever in view of its position opposite the new American defenses constructed at West Point. Here was a place where British ships could be stopped dead in the water, and the way to do it was to stretch an immense iron chain across the river from West Point to Constitution Island. The chain was forged of stout New Jersey iron (a portion of it can be seen at the state reservation at Ringwood, N.J.), floated across the river on barges, and securely anchored at either shore. Three redoubts and a battery were constructed on Constitution Island to protect the eastern end of the chain.

The chain did its job, and Constitution Island saw no further hostilities throughout the remaining five years of the war—no thanks to Benedict Arnold, who tried to hand over West Point and related defenses to the British in 1780. When the war ended in 1783, the barracks that had been built on the island were decommissioned, and civilian calm returned to this isolated spot on the Hudson.

Constitution Island gained fame in the nineteenth century as the home of the Warner sisters, Susan (1819–85) and Anna (1824–1915). Under pseudonyms, the two sisters wrote a total of 106 books, collaborating on 18 of them. Susan Warner is most famous for her novel *Wide, Wide World,* which was on the Civil War era's best-seller list (second in popularity only to *Uncle Tom's Cabin).* Anna Warner wrote the words to the famous hymn "Jesus Loves Me." Part of the present-day tour of the island is a visit to the Warners' house, fifteen rooms of which are furnished in the Victorian style of the Warner sisters' heyday. A guide takes visitors through the house, while the rest of the tour consists of a walk to and around the ruined fort.

Constitution Island is open to guided tours from mid-June through the end of September. Boats leave West Point South Dock at 1:00 and 2:00 P.M. Wednesday and Thursday afternoons. Fare and admission to the house and fort are $5 for adults; $4 for senior citizens and students; and $2 for children under 5. For information, contact the Constitution Island Association, Box 41, West Point, NY 10996, (914) 446–8676. Reservations must be made in advance.

Orange County comprises the southwestern portion of the Catskills, just north of the New Jersey state line. This is an area known for its fine standardbred horses, and it is quite fittingly the home of the **Hall of Fame of the Trotter and Trotting Horse Museum.** Standardbreds are the horses of the harness track, and Orange County is not only the home of some of the greatest

Hall of Fame of the Trotter, Goshen

standardbreds (including the legendary Hambletonian, sire of virtually all of today's trotters) but of the 153-year-old Historic Race Track, the only sporting site in the United States to have gained the status of a Registered National Historic Landmark.

Adjacent to the Historic Track is what appears to be a lovely Tudor mansion, a half-timbered structure actually built as the Good Time Stable. In 1951 the stable became the home of the Trotting Horse Museum, in which the history of American harness racing is told through a series of exhibits housed in the former box stalls. In addition to antique sulkies and tack, the displays include numerous fine examples of equestrian art, among them the famous Currier and Ives print of Hambletonian himself (1849–76).

The Hall of Fame of the Trotter honors the greats of harness racing—trainers, breeders, owners, and drivers. They're immortalized not by flat bronze plaques but by colorful, lifelike statuettes showing them in the garb of their professions.

The Hall of Fame of the Trotter and Trotting Horse Museum, 240 Main Street, Goshen, NY 10924, (914) 294–6330, is open Monday through Saturday, 10:00 A.M. to 5:00 P.M.; Sundays noon to 5:00 P.M.; and holidays, noon to 5:00 P.M. Closed Christmas, Thanksgiving, and New Year's Day. Admission is $1.50 for adults, $.50 for children.

Getting from one place to another quickly and with panache is an American preoccupation. In the nineteenth century a fast trotting horse might have done the trick; in the twentieth, we have the option of zipping along on or off the ground. If you like the idea of slipping silently through the air and didn't get your chance at the National Soaring Museum in Elmira (see chapter 3, Finger Lakes region), you'll find another opportunity in the southern Catskills at **Wurtsboro Airport,** near the intersection of Routes 17 and 209.

Established in 1927, Wurtsboro bills itself as the oldest soaring site in the nation. The Airport's Flight Service is the largest soaring school in the United States, offering lessons for people with no flight experience as well as for those licensed to fly power planes. For the casual visitor, however, the big attraction is the program of demonstration rides. After being towed aloft by a single-engine Cessna, you'll glide high above the Catskills with an FAA-rated commercial pilot at the stick. The ride lasts fifteen to twenty minutes and costs only $30. For $5 more, you can turn your joyride into an introductory lesson, with instructions in fundamental principles and basic flight controls.

Wurtsboro Airport and Flight Service, Wurtsboro, NY 12790, (914) 888–2791, is open daily, all year, 9:00 A.M. to dusk, weather permitting.

Back on the ground in the old Hudson Valley town of New Paltz, we encounter one of those odd superlatives, something you might never have devoted a moment's curiosity to but which is nonetheless fascinating once discovered. This is **Huguenot Street,** the oldest street in America that still has its original houses. Think about it; find a street where each building lot has had only one house upon it, and chances are you're in a 1950s subdivision. But the stone houses on Huguenot Street were built between 1692 and 1712, and they'll look good for at least another 300 years.

Persecuted by the Catholic majority in their native France and displaced by the incessant religious warfare of the seventeenth century, many Huguenots—peaceful members of a Protestant sect—came to southern New York in pursuit of freedom and tolerance. In 1677 twelve of their number purchased the lands around present-day New Paltz from the Esopus Indians and built log huts as their first habitations. The name of their village is taken from "die Pfalz," a section of Germany's Rhine-Palatinate region where they had formerly taken refuge.

As the twelve pioneers and their families prospered, they decided to build more permanent dwellings. And permanent they were: Here are five perfectly preserved houses, with additions that were built on by the settlers' descendants over the years. Only one, the 1692 Deyo House, was substantially remodeled, but even its 1890 wood-frame Queen Anne-style upper stories rest upon the solid stone foundations laid by its builder. The DuBois Fort, a handsome stone structure with a broad veranda and covered balcony, is now used as a restaurant. All of the houses are maintained by the Huguenot Historical Society, which manages a schedule of tours Wednesday through Sunday from Memorial Day weekend through September. Tours are available at varying rates and durations, ranging from a complete 2¼-hour tour of all of the houses and church (the houses are filled with period antiques) to short, one-house tours. For information, contact the Huguenot Society, P.O. Box 339, New Paltz, NY 12561, (914) 255–1660 or (914) 255–1889.

Just north of New Paltz, at High Falls, is a museum dedicated to a great work of engineering brought about because of an energy crisis. No, this one had nothing to do with OPEC or Iranian crude—it was the crisis in coal supply brought about by America's 1812–14 war with Great Britain. When the two countries were at peace, the United States imported soft coal from England. But when hostilities broke out, the supply was cut off, and entrepreneurs on this side of the Atlantic scrambled to find a substitute. Two of them were the Wurts brothers, Maurice and William, who figured that a canal was the way to bring Pennsylvania anthracite (hard coal) from the mines to New York City and vicinity, thus avoiding future shortages brought about by depending on foreign suppliers.

The two men formed the Delaware and Hudson Canal Company in 1825, with the stated purpose of linking Honesdale, Pennsylvania, with the Hudson River port of Eddyville, New York. The surveying and engineering of the 100-mile-plus route was han-

Abraham Hasbrouck House, New Paltz

dled by Benjamin Wright, chief engineer of the Erie Canal. The D&H Canal was completed in 1828 and enlarged and deepened to accommodate heavier traffic between 1847 and 1852. A lot of coal came down in barges along the old route, but the company that built it made a bold move in 1829 that would soon doom canals and the way of life they represented. In that year, the company began to work its gravity-operated rail line between Honesdale and Carbondale, Pennsylvania, with a new English contraption called a steam locomotive. Except for a few weedy stretches, the canal is gone—but the Delaware and Hudson Railroad survives to this day.

The **Delaware and Hudson Canal Museum** is the institution established to tell the story of the old canal, and it does so not merely through glassed-in exhibits but by preserving the extant structures, channel, and locks in the High Falls vicinity. There are five locks at High Falls—16, 17, 18, 19, and 20. The D&H Canal Historical Society has done whatever restoration and preservation work is possible on the locks and has linked canal sites in the area with a system of hiking trails. The museum building itself is near Locks 16 and 17 on Mohonk Road.

The Delaware and Hudson Canal Museum, Mohonk Road, High Falls, NY 12440, (914) 687–9311, is open Memorial Day weekend through Labor Day, Thursday through Monday, 11:00 A.M. to 5:00 P.M.; Sunday 1:00 to 5:00 P.M. Also open weekends in May, September, and October, Saturday, 11:00 A.M. to 5:00 P.M. and Sunday, 1:00 to 5:00 P.M. A small donation is requested.

The prodigious industrial expansion made possible by canals and railroads in the America of the nineteenth century was often accomplished at the expense of the natural environment, a phenomenon that persists in our own day. Fortunately, the 1800s also produced great pioneers of the conservationist spirit, whose writings and example point the way for those who continue their struggle today. Among them, of course, are the great Californian John Muir, and his equally dedicated near-contemporary John Burroughs, a native New Yorker who wrote twenty-five books on natural history and the philosophy of conservation. In 1895 Burroughs built a rustic log hideaway in the woods outside the village of West Park, barely 2 miles from the west bank of the Hudson. He called it **Slabsides,** and it is a National Historic Landmark today.

Burroughs, whose permanent home was only a mile and a half away, came to his little retreat to think, to write, and to quietly observe his natural surroundings. John Muir came here to talk with Burroughs, as did Theodore Roosevelt and Thomas Edison. They sat around the fire on log furniture of Burroughs's own manufacture, much of it still in the cabin.

Slabsides, which was deeded to the John Burroughs Association after the author's death in 1921, now stands within the 180-acre John Burroughs Sanctuary, a pleasant woodland tract that froms a most fitting living monument to his memory. The sanctuary is open all year; on the third Saturday in May and the first Saturday in October, the John Burroughs Association holds an open house at Slabsides from 11:00 A.M. to 4:00 P.M. In addition to an opportunity to see the cabin, the special days include informal talks and nature walks. Admission is free. For further information, write the Association at 15 West 77th Street, New York, NY 10024, or call (914) 384–6813 or (914) 255–0108.

Now we're going to the Broncks. No, it's not the wrong chapter—nor the wrong spelling. *Bronck* was the family name of one of the original clans of Swedish settlers in new Amsterdam and the Hudson Valley. The farmstead of Pieter Bronck, who settled on the west bank of the Hudson near what is now Coxsackie, today makes up the **Bronck Museum.**

It's one thing to have a surviving seventeenth-century house, but it is the great good fortune of the Greene County Historical Society, owner of the Bronck Museum, to be in possession of an entire farm dating from those early years of settlement. The reason the Bronck property has come down virtually intact is that eight generations of the family lived there, working the farm, until Leonard Bronk Lampman willed the acreage and buildings to the Society. Thus we get to appreciate not only the oldest of the farm buildings but also all of the barns, utility buildings, and furnishings acquired over several centuries of prosperity and familial expansion. What it all amounts to is an object lesson in the changes in style, taste, and sophistication that took place between the seventeenth and nineteenth centuries.

The original stone house on the property was built by Pieter Bronck himself in 1663. In 1685 Bronck built the stone west wing. The adjacent brick house, which reflects a more refined style, was built by a newer, more affluent generation of Broncks in 1738. In 1792 modifications to the original stone dwelling had to be made following a devastating storm, thus leaving us with examples of the early Federal mode. The little detached kitchen, opposite the main house in the rear courtyard, is also Federal in spirit.

Of the barns on the property, the most unusual is a thirteen-sided structure typical of a fad for multisided barns and homes in the mid-1800s. This and the Victorian horse barn contain antique agricultural equipment and horse-drawn vehicles, while the houses themselves are a repository of furniture from the Federal through Victorian eras, much of it having belonged to the Broncks. Of special note are the paintings by important members of the Hudson River School, including Thomas Cole (Cole memorabilia is also on display here) and John Frederick Kensett.

The Bronck Museum, Pieter Bronck Road (off Route 9W), (518) 731–8862 or (518) 731–6490 (mailing address: Greene County Historical Society, RD, Coxsackíe, NY 12051), is open from the last Sunday in June through the Sunday before Labor Day, Tuesday through Saturday, 10:00 A.M. to 5:00 P.M. (closed noon to 1:00 P.M.). Sunday hours are 2:00 to 6:00 P.M. Admission, including scheduled guided tours, is $2.50 for adults, $1 for children 12–15;

and \$.50 for children 5–11. Group tours, by prior arrangement, are available from May 30 through September 30.

If you're heading west from the Hudson Valley into the upper Catskills, a stop at the **Durham Center Museum** in East Durham provides an instructive look at the things a small community finds important—in many ways, this museum is archetypical of the "village attics" that dot the land, and travelers could do worse than to take an occasional poke into one of these institutions. At the Durham Center Museum, which is housed in a circa-1825 one-room schoolhouse and several newer adjacent buildings, the collections run to Indian artifacts, portions of local petrified trees, old farm tools, and mementos of the 1800 Susquehanna Turnpike and 1832–40 Canajoharie-Catskill Railroad, both of which passed this way. (The former was more successful than the latter, as a wooden rail from the C-C line, on display here, might lead you to suspect.) There is also a collection of Rogers Groups, those plaster statuette tableaux that decorated Victorian parlors and played on bourgeois heartstrings before Norman Rockwell was born. Finally, don't miss the collection of bottled sand specimens from around the world, sent by friends of the museum. If you're planning a trip to some far-off spot not represented on these shelves, don't hesitate to send some sand.

The Durham Center Museum, Route 145, East Durham, NY 12423, (518) 239–8461, is open Memorial Day through Labor Day, Wednesday through Thursday and on weekends, 12:30 to 4:00 P.M. Admission is \$1 for adults; \$.25 for children under 12. Groups are welcome by appointment April through October. Genealogical researchers are welcome year-round by appointment.

While spending a summer day in East Durham, drop in at another local institution with a far more specialized collection. This is **Richter's Butterfly Museum,** a small monument to one man's lifelong interest in lepidoptera. Max Richter was born in Germany, where even as a young boy he was fascinated with butterflies. When he moved to East Durham in 1932, he named his new country property Butterfly Farm. Here he raised butterflies, mounted them, and even made the mounted specimens into plaques. He opened his museum in 1953 and took great pride in showing his vast collection of butterflies to visitors over the next three decades. Mr. Richter passed away in 1984 at the age of one-hundred, but his museum remains open under the curatorship of his daughter, Helen Richter Kruppenbacher. She presides over an expanded institution that even houses collections of beetles and seashells, along with a gift shop selling *objets d' art* made from real butterflies.

The Butterfly Museum, Wright Street, East Durham, NY 12423, (518) 634–7759, is open during July and August on Wednesday, Thursday, and weekends, 2:00 to 5:00 P.M..

Roxbury, New York, is where we again come into contact with the naturalist John Burroughs. He may have spent much of the last decades of his life at Slabsides, down on the Hudson, but it was here in Roxbury that he was born in 1837 and here where he spent the last ten summers of his life at Woodchuck Lodge. He was buried here, in a field adjacent to the lodge, on April 2, 1921. The gravesite and the nearby "Boyhood Rock" that he had cherished as a lad are now part of **Burroughs Memorial State Historic Site.**

The Burroughs Memorial is unique among historic sites, in that its chief feature (apart from the grave and the rock) is simply a field, surrounded by forests and the rolling Catskill hills. This is as fine a memorial as one could possibly imagine for a man who once said about the Catskills, "Those hills comfort me as no other place in the world does—It is home there."

Burroughs Memorial, off Route 30 (take Hardscrabble Road to Burroughs Road), Roxbury, NY 12474, (315) 492–1756, is open during daylight hours from April to November 1. Admission is free. Woodchuck Lodge is frequently open to visitors on weekends during the summer.

Many of John Burroughs's modern-day spiritual descendants use the term *appropriate technology* to refer to renewable, non-polluting sources of energy. Over in the northwestern Catskills town of East Meredith, the **Hanford Mills Museum** celebrates one of the oldest of these so-called alternative-energy sources, the power of running water harnessed to a wheel. Kortright Creek at East Meredith has been the site of water-powered mills since the beginning of the nineteenth century, and the main building on the museum site today was built in 1820. In those days of clearing forests for farmland, lumber milling was a big local industry, and a good many of the older wooden structures in the East Meredith area were built with stock milled here.

The old mill became the Hanford Mills in 1860, when David Josiah Hanford bought the operation. During the eighty-five years in which it owned the mill, the Hanford family expanded its output to include flour and feed milling and the manufacture of utilitarian woodenware for farms and small industries. The mill complex grew to incorporate eight buildings on ten acres, all clustered around the mill pond. Sold in 1945 to Joseph, Michael, and Frank Pizza, all long-time workers for the Hanfords, the mill continued in operation until 1967.

Contrary to what appropriate-technology buffs might prefer, water power was not always the exclusive source of energy at the Hanford Mills. Steam, internal combustion, and electric motors all had their day here—but in 1899, when the lights went on in East Meredith for the first time, the electricity came from a hydro plant installed at Hanford Mills.

Not long after its final closing in the '60s Hanford Mills reopened as a museum. What could be a more perfect setup? Much of the original nineteenth-century equipment was still in place and in good working order. Today's visitors can watch lumber being cut on a big circular saw and shaped with smaller tools, all powered by the waters of Kortright Creek. At the heart of the operation is a 10-by-12-foot water wheel, doing what water wheels have done since before recorded history.

A tour of the museum includes a look at all of the woodworking operations, plus the shingle-making exhibit, located in a separate building, and a display of antique agricultural and woodworking equipment. At the museum store, you can buy wooden items made on the premises with the water-powered tools.

The Hanford Mills Museum, intersection of County Routes 10 and 12, East Meredith, NY 13757, (607) 278–5744, is open May 1 to October 31, daily, 10:00 A.M. to 5:00 P.M. Admission is $3 for adults; and $1.50 for children.

Off the Beaten Path in New York City and Long Island

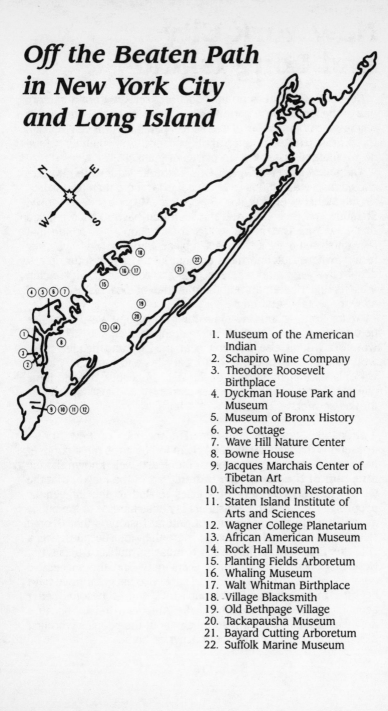

1. Museum of the American Indian
2. Schapiro Wine Company
3. Theodore Roosevelt Birthplace
4. Dyckman House Park and Museum
5. Museum of Bronx History
6. Poe Cottage
7. Wave Hill Nature Center
8. Bowne House
9. Jacques Marchais Center of Tibetan Art
10. Richmondtown Restoration
11. Staten Island Institute of Arts and Sciences
12. Wagner College Planetarium
13. African American Museum
14. Rock Hall Museum
15. Planting Fields Arboretum
16. Whaling Museum
17. Walt Whitman Birthplace
18. Village Blacksmith
19. Old Bethpage Village
20. Tackapausha Museum
21. Bayard Cutting Arboretum
22. Suffolk Marine Museum

New York City and Long Island

New York City needs no introduction—certainly not a cursory one of the length we're permitted here—except to note that this is where the most beaten of the state's paths converge. With one top-echelon attraction after another packed into the city, where do we find the lesser-known places of interest?

The answer is everywhere. One of the first things the traveler should realize about this city is that it is far more than a backdrop for the Statue of Liberty, the Metropolitan Museum of Art, Yankee Stadium, and their like. And natives often have to be reminded that New York isn't just a vast and cacophonous machine that reinvents itself daily. It is, in fact, a place with nearly 400 years of history, where Dutch farmers and quirky poets and future presidents have lived, and where people are concerned with Indian artifacts and Tibetan art and the minutiae of local history as well as with capital-C Culture.

As for Long Island, the main thing for people who don't live here to remember is that it's worth going to even if it isn't on the way to anything else. Starting near the city and heading east, we'll visit an assortment of historical sites and museums, along with places that remind us of the natural beauty and maritime flavor of Long Island before fast carpentry and fast food transformed so much of it into a vast suburb.

Of all the first-rank museums in the city of New York—institutions that can lay justified claim to being the most comprehensive of their kind—perhaps the least well known is the **Museum of the American Indian.** Part of the reason that the world's largest repository of articles related to the indigenous peoples of the Western Hemisphere is not as familiar to the public as, say, the American Museum of Natural History is that George Heye, its founder and director for more than four decades, was a collector first and by no means a museum publicist at all. But Heye has been dead for thirty years now, and the successive administrations that have come to supervise his great trove have been far more oriented to the public. It's time to become better acquainted with the Museum of the American Indian, because nowhere else can we learn so much about the peoples who first called North America and South America home.

Baldwin

**Carved Wooden Mask Inlaid with Shell.
Opiro Mound, Okla. A.D. 1200–1600**

George Heye was an heir to an oil fortune who early in his life worked as a railroad construction engineer in the Southwest. In 1897 he bought the first of his Indian artifacts, a contemporary Navajo buckskin shirt, and from that point went on to develop a collecting mania that encompassed all things native from Alaska to Tierra del Fuego. He bought items that had just been made (including, it is said, the clothes off Indians' backs), and he bought archaeological finds dating from long before the European discovery of America. Heye founded his museum in 1916, and it opened to the public six years later. At that stage the collector owned some four hundred thousand objects; today, the museum has more than a million individual items.

Exhibits at the Museum of the American Indian are arranged geographically, according to the regions inhabited by the major indigenous peoples of North America and South America. The first floor contains artifacts related to the North American tribes of the Great Lakes, Eastern woodlands, prairies, and high plains. The North American ethnology collection continues on the second floor, with Western, Southwestern, Canadian, and Eskimo exhibits; here also is the North American archaeology section. The third floor is given over to archaeological and ethnological exhibits representing Central America and South America and the West Indies.

An interesting feature of the Museum of the American Indian is that in addition to its strong generic holdings representing entire tribes and cultures (Pueblo pottery, tropical featherwork, wampum, South American silver jewelry, and much more), there are numerous items associated with individuals—Sitting Bull's war club, Crazy Horse's feather headdress, and Tecumseh's tomahawk, among others. Much of the collection, of course, must be kept in storage, accessible to those scholars who make appointments to visit the institution's research branch in the Bronx. But the astounding variety of material that is on display should surely convince visitors that this is *the* museum of the peoples of the New World.

The Museum of the American Indian, Broadway at 155th Street, New York, NY 10032, (212) 283–2420, is open Tuesday through Saturday, 10:00 A.M. to 5:00 P.M.; Sunday 1:00 to 5:00 P.M. Admission is $3 for adults; $2 for students and senior citizens with ID. Native Americans and members are admitted free.

New York City is the home of the world's largest Jewish community, a fact that necessitates an extensive infrastructure for providing kosher food and drink. Part of the picture is a winery called **Schapiro's,** located not in the Finger Lakes but right downtown on Rivington Street. Schapiro's makes the rich, heavy, sweet kosher wine, the traditional Passover drink made from Concord grapes—a product that, the firm boasts, you can almost "cut with a knife." The Schapiro list also includes sweet domestic standbys made from cherries and blackberries, along with tokay, sauterne, and white Concord.

The real revelations among the Schapiro offerings, though, are the imported Italian and French kosher wines. Did you know you could buy a kosher Valpolicella? How about a Sauvignon blanc, bottled at the Chateau in Bordeaux—also kosher. There are even a couple of kosher champagnes, straight from Epernay.

Schapiro's sells all of these wines and more, but the fun of a visit to the company lies not only in picking from the list but in taking an actual urban winery tour and seeing how Schapiro's own wines are made. The address is 126 Rivington Street, New York, NY 10002, (212) 674-4404. Tours are given every Sunday, 11:00 A.M. to 4:00 P.M. Admission is $1 per person.

Back in Buffalo a couple of chapters ago, we saw where the most momentous turn in Theodore Roosevelt's life took place—the house where he was inaugurated president of the United States. Here in the city you can see where his life began, at the **Theodore Roosevelt Birthplace National Historic Site.** The building that stands here today is a faithful replica of the brownstone row house in which TR was born on October 27, 1858. It was built following the ex-president's death in 1919, replacing a nondescript commercial building that had gone up only three years before, when the original Roosevelt home was torn down.

When Theodore Roosevelt's parents moved into the house at 28 East 20th Street in 1854, this was a fashionable residential neighborhood. But nineteenth-century New York was a city in constant flux, even more than the metropolis we know today, and by 1872, the year the Roosevelts left for a year in Europe, the upper middle class to which they belonged was already decamping for addresses farther to the north. When the family returned from abroad, they resettled not on 20th Street but way uptown on West 57th.

Open to the public since 1923, and a National Historic Site since 1963, the reconstructed Roosevelt home is furnished in much the same style—and with many of the same articles— familiar to the sickly lad who lived here for the first fourteen

Qui Plantavit Curabit

The Roosevelt Arms, Theodore Roosevelt Birthplace, Manhattan

years of his life. The rosewood furniture of the master bedroom belonged to the senior Roosevelts, and the crib and rush-seated chair in the nursery are believed to have been Teddy's. (Actually, in those days he was called "Teedie.") The president's widow and his surviving sisters helped with the reconstruction, recalling room layouts, furniture placement, and even interior color schemes. The result is not only a careful study of the environment that produced the scholar and improbable athlete who would become a rancher, police commissioner, Rough Rider, New York governor, and president, but of the life-style of New York's more comfortable burghers in the middle of the last century. Finally, the "new" Roosevelt house stands in stubborn contrast to the modern buildings that surround it, reminding us of just how completely the neighborhoods of New York have thrown off one persona after another.

The Theodore Roosevelt Birthplace National Historic Site, 28 East 20th Street, New York, NY 10003, (212) 260–1616, is open Wednesday through Sunday, 9:00 A.M. to 5:00 P.M. Admission is $1.

Theodore Roosevelt was the descendant of Claus Van Rosenvelt, who came to New Amsterdam from Holland in the 1640s. At about the same time another Dutch emigrant, Jan Dyckman, found his way to the fledgling colony by way of the German province of Westphalia. He settled in the then far-out-of-the-way village of New Haarlem, up at the northern tip of Manhattan Island, from which a trip down to Peter Stuyvesant's community near the Battery must have seemed a major expedition. Dyckman's descendants were important landholders here for generations. One of them, William Dyckman (1725–87) built a house on what is now Broadway and 204th Street just two years before his death. It still stands, and by dint of sheer endurance now has the honor of being the last eighteenth-century farmhouse on Manhattan Island.

The **Dyckman House,** donated to the city in 1915 by the daughters of the last Dyckman to live there, is a classic gambrel-roofed Dutch Colonial structure. With two full floors and an attic above a basement, it was substantial in its day—but remember, it was the main house of a sizable farm. In the fashion of the era, the winter kitchen was located in the basement, where the cooking fires would help to heat the house; here, today, are surviving examples of eighteenth-century cooking utensils as well as "modern" pieces from the 1800s. (The summer kitchen was kept out of the main building and occupied the small south wing. This portion of the Dyckman House is a survivor from an earlier structure that was destroyed during the Revolution.)

Furnishings in the Dyckman House include numerous family-associated items dating to the eighteenth century. For the most part, these are concentrated in the parlor and dining room on the first floor and in one of the five upstairs bedrooms. Another attraction for visitors is the small collection of Revolutionary artifacts excavated on the site and in the vicinity of the one-time farm, which was used as a camp by the British and Hessians who held New York throughout much of the war. A hut, representative of bivouac accommodations of the era, has been reconstructed behind the house.

The Dyckman House, 4881 Broadway, New York, NY 10034, is open Tuesday through Sunday, 11:00 A.M. to noon and 1:00 to 4:00 P.M. Closed holidays. Admission is $1. Guided tours of the museum and park, which cost $2, are by reservation only. Call the Metropolitan Historic Structures Association, (212) 304–9422.

And now, on to the U.S. mainland—to the only borough of the city of New York not located on an island. This is the Bronx, a place that ought to be recognized as more than the home of Yankee Stadium and the place you cross on Route 95 to get from New England to the George Washington Bridge. To get a handle on the story of this one-time suburban retreat that became one of New York's most densely populated residential districts, visit the **Museum of Bronx History.** The museum is housed in a building of a style and period not often encountered in a city that has torn down and rebuilt itself with as much abandon as has New York—a fieldstone house built in 1758, looking as if it would be more at home on a farm in Bucks County, Pennsylvania, than in the borough of endless row houses and apartment buildings.

The ivy-covered house, built by early Bronx settler Isaac Varian, contains both permanent and changing exhibits chronicling the roles played by the Bronx and Bronx people over the past three centuries. There's a lot to learn: For instance, the Bronx figured importantly in the American Revolution, particularly in the Battle of Pell's Point near present-day Pellham Bay Park. On October 12, 1776, 750 Continental troops under Col. John Glover so harassed Sir Harry Clinton's British landing force that George Washington was given precious time in which to complete his retreat to White Plains. No, the history of the Bronx did not begin with Babe Ruth, Lou Gehrig, and the coinage of the word *Bombers*.

The Museum of Bronx History, 3266 Bainbridge Avenue at 208th Street, Bronx, NY 10467, (212) 881–8900, is open Saturday, 10:00 A.M. to 4:00 P.M.; Sunday 1:00 to 5:00 P.M.; weekdays 9:00 A.M. to 5:00 P.M. by appointment. Admission is $1; children under 12 admitted free.

One chapter in Bronx history is an important part of American literary history as well. In 1846, a thirty-seven-year-old poet, short-story writer, and critic named Edgar Allan Poe rented a small wooden cottage now known as the **Poe Cottage,** in Poe Park, East Kingsbridge Road and the Grand Concourse, not far from the campus of Fordham University (in Poe's day, it was known as St. John's College). Part of the reason for his move was the fragile health of his wife; Fordham, Poe felt, was a more salubrious environment than the couple's former home of New York City. But Virginia Clemm Poe—who was also the writer's cousin— died of tuberculosis at the Bronx cottage early in 1847, leaving Poe in the state of despondency that accounted for his poem "Annabel Lee" and other melancholic verse.

Poe kept up his residence in the Bronx after his wife's death, drinking heavily and trying to keep up with his bills by delivering an occasional lecture. It was while returning from one of his lecture trips that Poe died in Baltimore in 1849.

Sometimes the world takes better care of dead poets' residences than it does of the poets while they are alive, and such was the case with Edgar Allan Poe. The rapidly growing Bronx quickly enveloped the Poe Cottage during the latter half of the nineteenth century, but in 1902 the city of New York dedicated a park in Poe's honor across the street from the house. The house was moved to the park eleven years later and has been open as a museum since 1917. Refurbished by the Bronx Society of Arts and Sciences and the Bronx County Historical Society to a close approximation of its appearance during the last three years of Poe's life, the cottage offers visitors a chance to see the room in which the poet wrote "Annabel Lee" and several of his other best-remembered poems and the room where Virginia Poe died. A visit to the Poe Cottage is also a chance to see what places like Fordham Village were like before the elevated railways made the Bronx first a suburb and then an integral part of urban New York.

The Edgar Allan Poe Cottage, Grand Concourse and East Kingsbridge Road, Bronx, NY 10458, (212) 881–8900, is open Wednesday through Friday, 9:00 A.M. to 5:00 P.M.; Saturday, 10:00 A.M. to 4:00 P.M.; Sunday, 1:00 to 5:00 P.M. An audiovisual presentation is shown throughout visiting hours. Admission is $1 for adults; children under 12 admitted free.

Not all of the Bronx was gobbled up by developers in the decades following Poe's brief stay. There are, of course, the green expanses of the New York Botanical and Zoological gardens, Van Cortlandt Park, and Pelham Bay Park. But a visit to the borough should also include a stop at **Wave Hill,** a 28-acre preserve in the Riverdale neighborhood at the northwest corner of the Bronx. Wave Hill is not wilderness but a section of the borough that remained in its natural state until the middle of the last century, when it was first acquired as a country estate. Today, it is the only one of the great Hudson River estates preserved for public use within the New York City limits.

In 1836 New York lawyer William Morris bought 15 acres of riverbank real estate in the Wave Hill area and built Wave Hill House, one of the two mansions that today grace the property, as a summer retreat. Thirty years later, the Morris tract was acquired by publisher William Appleton. Appleton remodeled the house and began developing the gardens and conservatories for which the property would become famous. The gardens were brought to their apogee, however, by financier George Perkins, who bought the estate in 1893 and increased its size to 80 acres, with a scattering of six fine houses including not only Wave Hill but also

Glyndor, which had been built by Oliver Harriman. (Burnt in 1927, Glyndor was rebuilt by Perkins's widow. "Glyndor II," as it is known, is still a part of the Wave Hill property.) Perkins's gardener was the talented Albert Millard. Under his direction, plantings on the estate were expanded to include eight additional greenhouses and exotic oriental trees.

The Perkins family owned Wave Hill until 1960, renting those houses they did not use themselves. One of their famous tenants was the conductor Arturo Toscanini, who later bought his own Riverdale house; earlier, Mark Twain had lived here during the last decade of his life. In 1960 the family gave the estate to the city of New York. Five years later, a corporation was authorized to manage the 28 remaining acres of the estate and develop a program of educational and cultural programs appropriate to the site.

The attractions of Wave Hill for today's visitor thus include an ambitious and successful calendar of art exhibits, concert series, outdoor dance performances, and special events. But the essential reason for a trip to the old estate remains its lovely grounds, some manicured and some an approximation of the wild state of this stretch of Bronx shoreline. There are 350 varieties of trees and shrubs, plus the wild and cultivated flowers planted in two greenhouses, in formal and informal gardens, and along the pathways of the estate. A 10-acre section of woods has even been the object of an effort to restore a native Bronx forest environment, complete with elderberries, witch hazel, and native grasses.

Wave Hill, 249th Street and Independence Avenue, Bronx, NY (675 West 252 Street, Bronx, NY 10471 is the mailing address), (212) 549–3200, is open daily 10:00 A.M. to 4:30 P.M. Admission is free weekdays; Saturdays and Sundays, $2 for adults; $1 for seniors and students; children 6 and under free. Tours are given each Sunday. Closed Christmas Day and New Year's Day.

The borough of Queens is New York's most residential neighborhood—or, rather, collection of neighborhoods, each retaining its own distinctive character. One such neighborhood is Flushing, best known to many non-native New Yorkers as the site of the 1939 and 1964 World's Fairs. The history of this district goes back well over 300 years, as a visit to the **Bowne House** will demonstrate.

John Bowne built the house that today bears his name in 1661. To get some idea of what the future outlying boroughs of New York were like in those days, consider that two years after the Bowne House was built, the town meeting of nearby Jamaica offered a bounty of seven bushels of corn for every wolf shot or otherwise done away with. But wolves weren't the only threat John Bowne faced. A Quaker, he openly challenged Governor Peter Stuyvesant's edict banning that religion by holding meetings of the Society of Friends in his kitchen. He was arrested and sent back to Europe in 1662 but came back to New York two years later after having been exonerated by the Dutch West India Company, managers of the New Amsterdam colony. The status of Dutch acceptance of religious dissent was by then practically a moot point, since Great Britain was soon to take over the colony. But Bowne's stand was nevertheless an important step toward the American predilection for religious freedom, an attitude enshrined in the U.S. Constitution 125 years later.

Now the oldest house in Queens, the Bowne House reflects not only the Dutch/English colonial style in which it was originally built but all of the vernacular styles with which it was modified over the years. The original three-room structure was expanded to include a parlor (the present-day "dining room") in 1680; the living room was added in 1696 and later paneled in the Georgian style. Extra space upstairs and a first floor rear room were created early in the nineteenth century by a raising of the roof.

Indoors, the Bowne House displays styles of furnishing and portrait painting as they developed over the first two centuries of its existence. Everything here belonged to the Bownes, making this property a unique documentation of one family's experience in New York virtually from the time of its founding to the beginning of the modern era.

The Bowne House, 37-01 Bowne Street, Flushing, NY 11354, (718) 359–0528, is open Tuesday, Saturday, and Sunday, 2:30 to 4:30 P.M.; also open July 4 to Labor Day, Tuesdays and Thursdays, 11:00 A.M. to 3:00 P.M.; closed mid-December to mid-January. Admission is $2 for adults; $.50 for children. Groups welcome on weekday afternoons; by appointment only.

A seventeenth-century Quaker going to a clandestine meeting at the Bowne House might seem to have little in common with a twentieth-century Tibetan Buddhist, but the two share a bond of persecution. One of the uglier aspects of the Maoist period in China was the annexation of Tibet and the suppression of its ancient culture and religion. Despite some recent liberalization on the part of the Chinese occupiers of Tibet, it is still an extremely difficult place to visit; and, ironically, those Westerners interested in Tibetan art and religious artifacts have learned to

Baldwin

Crowned Buddha, Marchais Center of Tibetan Art, Staten Island

rely on foreign rather than native Tibetan collections. One such collection is the **Jacques Marchais Center of Tibetan Art** on Staten Island.

If we were to expect to find a small museum of Tibetan art at all in New York City, we would expect it in the cultural polyglot of Manhattan rather than in residential Staten Island. But here on its hillside is the Tibetan Museum, itself resembling a small Tibetan Buddhist temple. It houses more than a thousand examples of Tibetan religious art—paintings, carved and cast statues, altars, and even musical instruments—each of which was created to aid in the meditation that is such an important part of Buddhism, especially as practiced in Tibet.

And who was Jacques Marchais? There was no Jacques Marchais—or rather, "he" was a woman named Jacqueline Norman Klauber who operated a Manhattan art gallery under the masculine French pseudonym. Klauber/Marchais had a lifelong interest in things Tibetan, nurtured in childhood when she would play with Tibetan figurines her great-grandfather had brought back from the Orient. She never traveled to Tibet, but she carefully added to her collection in the years before 1947, when she completed the two stone buildings that house the museum and opened them to the public. Later that year, Mrs. Klauber died.

With its terraced gardens, lily pond, and air of detachment and serenity, the Marchais Center is indeed an appropriate setting for the religious objects that make up the collection, representing centuries of Tibetan culture. Among the secular meditations to which they are conducive is the contemplation of the Chinese destruction of some five thousand temples and lamaseries in Tibet, each of them containing similar artifacts of a way of thinking that Chairman Mao did not tolerate.

The Jacques Marchais Center of Tibetan Art, 338 Lighthouse Avenue, Staten Island, NY 10306, (718) 987–3478, is open 1:00 to 5:00 P.M., Wednesday through Sunday, from April through November; hours for December through March are by appointment. Closed Memorial Day, July 4, Labor Day, Thanksgiving Day, and the Friday following Thanksgiving Day. Admission is $2.50 for adults; $2 for senior citizens; $1 for children. Group and school tours welcome; call for appointment.

Within walking distance of the Marchais Center is a collection of buildings representative of cultural continuity rather than upheaval and transplanting. **Richmondtown Restoration** is a collection of twenty-seven buildings, fourteen of them restored and open to the public, which remind us that Staten Island has a richer history than might be suggested by the tract houses and refineries that characterize the present-day borough of Richmond. Richmondtown seems like a country village far from the bustle of Manhattan, and with good reason—that's what it was, in the seventeenth and eighteenth centuries when these houses and community buildings were built. Among them are the "Voorlezer's (teacher's) house," a Dutch-era one-room school; an old county courthouse; a general store; and a farmhouse. Many of the buildings are staffed by craftspeople working with period equipment, turning out such things as handmade pottery, leatherwork, and handwoven textiles. White clapboard farmhouses dot the property's 100 acres, and a central museum houses exhibits of Staten Island-made products that reveal the history and diversity of New York's least-populous borough. There are special events at the Restoration throughout the year, many of them related to holidays, and nineteenth-century dinners are served during the summer.

Richmondtown Restoration, 441 Clark Avenue, Staten Island, NY 10306, (718) 351–1611, is open Monday through Friday, 10:00 A.M. to 5:00 P.M.; Saturday and Sunday, 1:00 to 5:00 P.M. Admission is $4 for adults; $2.50 for students, senior citizens, and children 6–18.

If you are sold on Staten Island by now, the next logical stop is the **Staten Island Institute of Arts and Sciences.** The Institute, headquartered in the small community of St. George not far from the Staten Island ferry slips, encompasses three separate locations: the Staten Island Museum, at the Stuyvesant Street headquarters; the William T. Davis Wildlife Refuge off Travis Avenue opposite the New Jersey shore; and High Rock Park Conservation Center, an 85-acre preserve at Rockland Avenue and Richmond Road near the center of the island.

The Staten Island Museum possesses impressive collections of art and natural-science materials. Although the work of Staten Island artists such as Jasper Cropsey and Guy Pene duBois is well represented, the American holdings range as well to names like John Sloan, Reginald Marsh, and Robert Henri. There are also small collections of Italian Renaissance paintings and Third World ethnographic art, American and European prints dating from the fifteenth century, and antique British and American silver.

The Museum's natural-science holdings are more specifically geared to the Staten Island environment. Here are more than twenty thousand specimens: fossils, geological samples, insects, Indian relics, botanical material, and much more.

Because of limited exhibition space (a situation expected to be relieved in the early 1990s), the Staten Island Museum currently presents only special exhibits drawn from its permanent holdings, instead of attempting to keep the bulk of its collections in view.

The Institute's two nature preserves are perhaps the best sort of "display" relating to Staten Island's place in the natural world. The Davis Refuge consists of salt marsh, freshwater swamp, and both dry and wet woodlands. Named after a prominent entomologist who helped found the Institute, the refuge—though surrounded by landfill and development—continues to provide a haven for native and transplanted plant species, small animals such as muskrat, and numerous bird species. High Rock Park occupies higher ground, mostly hardwood forest with a swamp and several glacial ponds. Three specially planted areas are of particular interest. These are the Sensory Garden (fragrant and textured herbs, with Braille identification); the Centennial Spring Wildflower Garden (native forest plants); and the Interpretive Fern Garden, with local species identified.

The Staten Island Institute of Arts and Sciences (Staten Island Museum), 75 Stuyvesant Place, Staten Island, NY 10301, (718) 727–1135, is open Tuesday through Saturday, from 9:00 A.M. to 5:00 P.M.; Sunday, 1:00 to 5:00 P.M. Admission is charged. Museum personnel can direct visitors to the two outdoor facilities and provide maps and interpretive brochures.

Say "planetarium" in New York City, and people will almost always assume that you mean the famous Hayden Planetarium at the American Museum of Natural History. But there's a planetarium on Staten Island, too. It's the **Wagner College Planetarium,** opened in 1970. Public shows at the planetarium are offered each Sunday at 3:00 and 7:30 P.M., and Saturday at 11:15 A.M. (The planetarium is closed in August, and Sunday shows only are scheduled from May through July.) Each month, the projection is changed to emphasize a different astronomical topic. An item of note: The Wagner College Planetarium not only shows the stars, it's powered by one. This is the world's first solar-powered planetarium.

Wagner College Planetarium is on the campus at Grymes Hill, Staten Island, NY 10301. Telephone (718) 390–3100 for further information.

East of New York City, beyond the borders of the boroughs of Brooklyn and Queens, Long Island stretches from the populous cities and towns of Nassau County to the beaches and New England-style villages of Suffolk County. Beginning in the Nassau County city of Hempstead, our first stop is the **African American Museum.**

Founded in 1970 under the auspices of the Nassau County Department of Recreation and Parks in response to growing awareness of the contributions of blacks on Long Island, the Black History Exhibit Center recently changed its name, to the African American Museum, and its emphasis, to include interpretive exhibits of traditional and contemporary native African culture as well as local American black history and lore.

As the museum's 1985 exhibit "The World of Our Grandparents: African-Americans on Long Island 1880s–1920s" demonstrated, the black experience in New York State is by no means concentrated in New York City, nor is it a phenomenon largely associated with twentieth-century migrations from the South. A hundred years ago and more, blacks were farming, whaling, and working at crafts and small businesses on Long Island. Their ancestry, in many cases, dated back to the seventeenth- and eighteenth-century days when slavery—though not as wide-spread as it would become in the South—was still practiced in New York and the New England states.

The African American Museum tells the story of Long Island's blacks not only through displays of photographs and artifacts but through a lively program of lectures, community workshops, and performing arts. Local artistic talent is especially promoted. African-oriented exhibits and special programs have included recent shows devoted to West African crafts, art from Sierra Leone, African toys, and black artistic expression in South Africa.

The African American Museum, 110 North Franklin Street, Hempstead, NY 11550, (516) 485–0470, is open Tuesday through Saturday, 9:00 A.M. to 4:45 P.M.; Sunday 12:45 to 4:45 P.M. Closed Monday and holidays. Admission is free.

Another Hempstead attraction is not really in Hempstead but in the south-shore village of Lawrence, just across the New York City limits from Far Rockaway, Queens. This is **Rock Hall,** a 1767 mansion built by Tory merchant Josiah Martin.

Rock Hall represents the high-water mark of late Georgian architecture in this part of the United States, particularly in its interior detailing. The paneling and mantels, as well as much of the eighteenth- and early-nineteenth-century furniture and the replica of a colonial kitchen (the original kitchen was in an outbuilding), came down virtually unchanged to our own time largely because of the infrequency with which the house changed hands over its 220-year history. Josiah Martin's family, having come through the Revolution none the worse for being on wrong side, lived here until 1823. The following year, Thomas Hewlett bought Rock Hall; his family lived in the mansion for more than a century after his death in 1841. In 1948 the Hewletts gave the place to the Town of Hempstead—presumably then a larger municipal entity—for use as a museum, and so it has remained. Only two families have lived here over the past two centuries plus, which is why it looks as if one of their number has just gone out to pick up some Madeira.

Rock Hall Museum, 199 Broadway, Lawrence, NY 11559, (516) 239–1157, is open April 1 through November 30, Monday through Saturday, 10:00 A.M. to 4:00 P.M.; noon to 4:00 P.M. on Sunday. Closed Tuesday. Admission is free.

Up on the north shore of Long Island, in Oyster Bay, **Planting**

Whaling Museum, Sag Harbor

Fields Arboretum is the legacy of William Robertson Coe, a British-born insurance magnate who purchased this property in 1913. Coe immediately set about making his 409-acre estate into as complete a farm-garden-arboretum as possible. He began building greenhouses in 1914 (Coe Hall, the great house on the property, did not go up until 1919–21) and imported his camellia collection in 1917. The camellias couldn't make it through a Long Island winter, so a special greenhouse was built for them. Coe set up a working dairy and kept pigs and chickens as well. (Milk and produce from Planting Fields graced Coe's table in Manhattan when he wasn't in residence at the estate and were donated to the needy during the Depression.)

But it was trees and shrubs that most commanded Coe's attention, and they were the subjects of some of his greatest extravagances. The copper beech on the mansion's north lawn, for instance, was moved here from Massachusetts by barge and a team of seventy-two horses when it was already 60 feet high. Working with master landscape gardeners such as A. Robeson Sargent, and James Dawson of Olmsted Brothers, Coe created grand allees of trees designed to frame the views from the house and established rambling azalea walks. As late as the 1950s, in the last years of his life, Coe planted the rhododendron park, which remains one of the outstanding features of Planting Fields.

Coe died in 1955, six years after arranging for the state to assume ownership of Planting Fields after his death. He also left a generous endowment, which, along with funds appropriated by the state and raised by the private Friends of Planting Fields, helps to keep the arboretum, greenhouses, and buildings on the property in their current excellent state of maintenance. The decades since Coe's death have even seen new additions to the plantings here. One is the "synoptic garden," so called because it represents a synopsis of the ornamental plants appropriate for Long Island and the greater New York area. The plants are even arranged in alphabetical order, at least one for each letter.

Other attractions not to be missed on a visit to Planting Fields are the dwarf conifer garden, hollies, rose arbor, and main greenhouse. The latter is a tropical microclimate of coffee, banana, pineapple, citrus, and even date palms. There are concerts in the Haybarn (write to the address below for a schedule), and from April through September, visitors can tour Coe Hall itself Monday through Friday, 1:00 to 3:30 P.M.

Planting Fields Arboretum, Box 58 (off Mill River Road), Oyster Bay, NY 11771, (516) 922–9200, is open daily, 9:00 A.M. to 5:00 P.M. Admission is $1.50; from Labor Day through mid-April, it is charged on Saturdays, Sundays, and holidays only. Admission is free for children under 12.

> "Tis advertised in Boston, New York and
>   Buffalo,
> Five hundred brave Americans a-whaling for
>   to go,
> Singing 'Blow, ye winds in the morning,
> Blow ye winds heigh-o,
> Heave away, haul away, and blow, winds,
>   blow.' "

So goes the old chantey.

But where would these brave whalers ship out from, once they had answered the call? Most often, they would go down to the sea at New Bedford or Nantucket; if they began their hard voyages on Long Island, most likely their home port would be Sag Harbor. But there were also smaller whaling ports on Long Island, one of which was the north-shore community of Cold Spring Harbor. Here today is the **Whaling Museum,** which celebrates the skills and adventures of the town's own whalers as well as those of other men who worked in this unique and arduous industry from colonial times through the nineteenth century.

Cold Spring Harbor was never a sizable whaling port. During its peak years, 1836 to 1862, the town's fleet numbered a total of only nine ships—although one of them, the *Sheffield* (in service from 1845 to 1859), was the largest whaler to use a Long Island harbor as its home port. Nevertheless, the Cold Spring fleet worked hard at whaling, sailing into the Atlantic and "around the Horn" into Pacific and Indian ocean waters in pursuit of sperm and bowhead whales, and even into the treacherous Arctic Ocean. As with whaling men from New Bedford and Nantucket and all the lesser ports, the hands who signed on at Cold Spring could expect to spend two or three years or more aboard their wooden ships, seagoing factories built for the hunting and processing of whales.

The Whaling Museum houses a large collection of the implements used in the whale "fishery," as it was known, despite the fact that the great beasts are mammals. Here are harpoons, lances, and the tools used in separating blubber from whale carcasses. A permanent exhibit, "Mark Well the Whale," details the history and impact of whaling on the locality. There are logbooks of whaling voyages and even an entire whaleboat, last used in 1913. Sixty of the museum's finest whalebone carvings and specimens of the famous scrimshaw engraving, practiced to relieve the monotony of long days at sea, are also on display in a new scrimshaw addition to the permanent exhibit, as are prints and paintings of ships, whales, and whalemen.

The Museum is admirably not solely dedicated to commemorating the human side of whaling; it also fosters knowledge of the enormous and intelligent creatures that the whalers so relentlessly pursued. The institution's policy is to condemn the industrialized whaling still practiced by a handful of countries and endorse conservation efforts. A cornerstone of conservation policy is education, and the Whaling Museum is a good place for children and adults alike to learn about the lives and habits of the largest, and in many ways the most threatened, of all the animals on earth.

The Whaling Museum, Box 25, Cold Spring Harbor, NY 11724, (516) 367–3418, is open daily from Memorial Day through Labor Day; closed Monday during the rest of the year. Hours are 11:00 A.M. to 5:00 P.M. Admission is $2 for adults; $1 for children 6–14; and $1 for senior citizens.

Several decades before the whaling industry at Cold Spring Harbor hit its stride, there was born in the nearby town of Huntington a boy who would become a printer, newspaperman, schoolteacher, Civil War nurse, Washington bureaucrat, and one of the greatest poets America has produced. Walt Whitman (1819–92) first saw daylight in a Huntington farmhouse built about 1816, which is today preserved as the **Walt Whitman Birthplace.**

Although Whitman's ancestors had lived in the area around Huntington since the mid-seventeenth century, the boy moved to Brooklyn with his family when he was only four years old. He came back after his apprenticeship as a journalist, though, and founded *The Long Islander,* a weekly newspaper that survives to this day. He also taught school in Huntington.

The house in which Walt Whitman was born is atypical (in interior architectural detail) of most farmhouses of the early nineteenth century, but like many of them it might have had little hope of surviving into the twenty-first, had not one of its first inhabitants gone on to become the "Good Grey Poet." In the early 1950s the Whitman Birthplace was about to be leveled by the advance of postwar suburban development, when Huntington residents held off the bulldozers and had the house placed under protective state ownership. It has been completely restored and is now a New York State Historic Site. It is administered by the Walt Whitman Birthplace Association.

The Walt Whitman Birthplace, 246 Old Walt Whitman Road, Huntington Station, NY 11746, (516) 427–5240, is open Wednesday through Friday, 1:00 to 4:00 P.M.; Saturday and Sunday, 10:00 A.M. to 4:00 P.M. Admission is free.

It was not Walt Whitman but his contemporary Henry Wadsworth Longfellow who wrote, "Under the spreading chestnut tree/The village smithy stands." Just a short hop east of Huntington, in Northport, stands an institution that either Whitman or Longfellow would easily recognize—a blacksmith shop. The **Vil-**

lage **Blacksmith** is a family enterprise, launched in 1977 by Bernard and Ann Reichert and their sons, James and William. Not many families start up blacksmith shops any more, but the Reicherts did it up right. They purchased an 1830 farmhouse that had served as a gas station, installed a forge, and set up shop selling handcrafted ironware made on the premises as well as items such as cast-iron and pewter reproductions. The output of the Reichert forge included fireplace tools, trivets, chandeliers, sconces, hooks—just about every sort of useful wrought ironware, some of its commissioned by the smithy's clientele as custom work.

The Village Blacksmith, 141 Main Street, Northport, NY 11768, (516) 757–3620, is open Monday through Saturday from 10:00 A.M. to 5:30 P.M.; Sunday, 11:00 A.M. to 5:00 P.M.

Returning to the inland center of Long Island, we find plentiful evidence of the relentless trend toward suburbanization that has characterized this place during the past forty years. But we also find an institution that has set as its goal the preservation of as much as possible of the old, rural Long Island way of life. **Old Bethpage Village Restoration** is a re-creation of the world as it was long before there was a Levittown or Long Island Expressway. In fact—at least as far as its buildings are concerned—it is the architectural equivalent of a wildlife preserve. Starting in the middle 1960s, the curators of the village (it's managed by the Nassau County Department of Recreation and Parks) began moving threatened colonial and early-nineteenth-century structures here, where they could be set up in a close approximation of a Long Island village of the Civil War era. There are now nearly fifty buildings on the site, all of them having been chosen to represent typical domestic, commercial, and agricultural structures of the era.

All of those buildings without people and activity would make for a rather dry museum, so Old Bethpage Village has been staffed with working artisans and craftspeople—you'll find a blacksmith at work in the blacksmith shop, farmers tilling the fields with horse-drawn plows, and housewives holding quilting bees. There's even an Old Bethpage Village militia, which will presumably come in handy if the place is ever attacked by a contingent from the Genesee Country Village or the Farmers' Museum at Cooperstown.

One engaging feature of life at Old Bethpage Village is the full calendar of seasonal events, all of them suggestive of the things people used to do at different times of the year back when there

Quilting in the Noon Inn, Old Bethpage

were different times of year, other than in terms of the weather. There are old-fashioned Valentine's Day celebrations, April town meetings, a late May sheep-shearing, a Fourth of July complete with speeches, a harvest festival called Long Island Fair, a November "political campaign" based on century-old candidacies, and a celebration of New Year holiday traditions (they're open evenings December. 26–30).

Old Bethpage Village Restoration, Round Swamp Road, Old Bethpage, NY 11804, (516) 420–5280, is open Tuesday through Sunday throughout the year. Hours from March through November are 10:00 A.M. to 5:00 P.M.; December through February, 10:00 A.M. to 4:00 P.M. Admission is $4 for adults; $2 for senior citizens and children 5–17.

Just south of Bethpage, on Long Island's south shore in Seaford, is a museum and preserve dedicated to life on the island as it was lived even before the era of farm and village life. The

Tackapausha Museum and Preserve is an 80-acre introduction to the ecology and natural history of the Northeast's coastal woodlands as they existed before human intervention. Well, at least before European intervention. Tackapausha is named after a sachem (chief) of Long Island's native Massapequa Indians, a group that by and large managed to live on this land without greatly affecting its wildlife, plant communities, or the balance of natural forces. But at least it can occasionally be said of our society that we can recognize the problems we cause and set aside places like this—not only for their own sake but for the important cause of educating subsequent generations.

The Tackapausha Museum is a small facility designed to serve as an introduction to the plants and animal life of the preserve itself. Exhibits explain the relationship between habitat groups, the differences between diurnal and nocturnal animals, and the changes in life patterns brought about by the different seasons. There is also a small collection of native animals, housed in as natural a setting as possible.

The preserve itself is a lovely piece of land, incorporating a variety of ecosystems. Here is one of the last stands of Atlantic white cedar on Long Island, along with deciduous forest, meadows, and wetlands. Red maple, white oak, and fields of wildflowers provide food and cover for more than forty species of birds and for small mammals such as muskrat and raccoon. A self-guiding trail (pick up the interpretive map at the museum) takes visitors through the different preserve environments.

The Tackapausha Museum and Preserve, Washington Avenue, Seaford, NY 11783, (516) 785–2802, is open daily, 10:00 A.M. to 4:45 P.M., except major holidays. Admission is $.25; free for children under 5 if accompanied by a parent.

Like Planting Fields in Oyster Bay, the south shore's **Bayard Cutting Arboretum** is another rich man's estate that has become a mecca for those who enjoy majestic trees and beautiful gardens. The arboretum, which is virtually adjacent to the state-managed Connetquot River Park, was once the property of one of New York City's ablest financial operators. William Bayard Cutting (1850–1912) was a lawyer, railroad director and president, banker, insurance executive, and philanthropist, noted for having built the first block of Manhattan tenements to feature indoor plumbing.

In his leisure time (whenever that might have been), Bayard Cutting enjoyed himself by improving his Long Island retreat. He built the sixty-eight-room Tudor mansion that stands on the arboretum grounds in 1886, with a few decorative touches by his friend Louis Comfort Tiffany. (Visitors can enter the mansion, the former breakfast room of which houses a well-maintained collection of mounted birds.) When it came to landscaping, Cutting placed a good deal of trust in another friend, the great Harvard botanist and silviculturist Charles Sprague Sargent. Together with none other than Frederick Law Olmsted, Sargent was responsible for much of the appearance of the Cutting estate and, subsequently, the arboretum.

The trees of the Cutting Arboretum are an interesting mix of native and imported species. There are exotics such as Algerian and blue Spanish firs and one of the world's largest Sargent weeping hemlocks. If it sounds as if coniferous species are a Cutting specialty, they are—although the arboretum's "pinetum," decimated by hurricane Gloria in 1985, is still being partially replanted as of this writing. Some irreplaceable trees were lost when that fierce storm hit the south shore of Long Island.

The Bayard Cutting Arboretum is an especially pleasant place for a quiet stroll, even for those not well versed in tree species. We all know azaleas and rhododendrons, and they grow here in profusion. The streams and pond, with their ducks and geese and graceful little footbridges, are reason enough to spend an afternoon at the Cutting.

The Bayard Cutting Arboretum, Route 27A, Oakdale, NY, (516) 581–1002, is open Wednesday through Sunday, 10:00 A.M. to 5:30 P.M. (4:30 when Eastern Standard Time is in effect). Admission is $3 per car; free from October through April.

Within a few miles of the Cutting Arboretum, on the Great South Bay that divides the barrier beach of Fire Island from the Long Island mainland, is the village of West Sayville, with its **Suffolk Marine Museum.** The whalers of Cold Spring Harbor were by no means the only brave Long Islanders to go down to the sea in ships to pursue their quarry; here in West Sayville, men went out into dangerous waters to harvest the more prosaic but nonetheless important oyster. The Marine Museum, in fact, includes a vintage 1907 restored oyster house and has among its holdings the largest collection of small craft on Long Island.

The oystermen's boats were among the most functionally beautiful of all wooden small craft. Two of the finest examples here are the 1888 schooner *Priscilla* and the 1923 sloop *Modesty,* both honored veterans of the oyster grounds. There is also a restored boatbuilder's shop, illustrative of the skill and care that went into the building of these essential commercial vessels. Other exhibits concentrate upon the tools of oystermen over the years.

It isn't all oysters at the Marine Museum. Displays of yachting and racing memorabilia, model boats, and artifacts related to the lifesaving service of the nineteenth century round out the museum's collections. Duck and other shorebird decoys, an integral part of American folk art in shoreline communities well into this century, are also on exhibit. In 1988 the Bayman's Cottage opened: Visitors are taken through it when guides are available. Exhibits in the kitchen, pantry, bedroom, and living room depict the style of living at the turn of the century.

Suffolk Marine Museum, Route 27A, West Sayville, NY 11796, (516) 567-1733, is open Monday through Saturday, 10:00 A.M. to 3:00 P.M.; Sunday, noon to 4:00 P.M. The museum is closed Mondays and Tuesdays during the winter months. Admission is free, but donations are appreciated.

Index

A

Adirondack Forest Preserve, 26
Adirondack Museum, 36, 37
Adirondack State Park, 26
African American Museum, 131, 132
Albany, 50, 51, 52
Albany Institute of History and Art, 50, 51
Alexandria Bay, 44
Algonquins, 39
Allegany State Park, 92
Allen, Ethan, 34, 35
Allentown (Buffalo), 96
Alling Coverlet Museum, 85, 86
Amherst, General Sir Jeffrey, 34, 36
Ancram, 16
Arcade and Attica Railroad, 101, 102
Arnold, General Benedict, 27, 52, 107
Auburn, 87, 88
Auriesville, 56
AWA Electronic Communications Museum, 81, 82

B

Baldwinsville, 89
Barnum, Phineas Taylor, 11
Baseball Hall of Fame, 59, 60
Bayard Cutting Arboretum, 139, 140
Beaver Lake Nature Center, 89
Bennington, Battle of, 22
Blue Mountain Lake, 36, 37
Boldt Castle, 43, 44
Borden, Gail, 11
Boscobel, 11, 12, *illus.,* 13
Bowne House, 126, 127
Brewster, 11
Bronck Museum, 113, 114
Bronx, 124, 125
Brown, John, 37, 38
Buffalo, 92, 96, 97, 98, 99, 100
Buffalo Museum of Science, 99, 100

Burgoyne, General John, 22, 27, 29, 34, 52, 63
Burrough, Memorial State Historic Site, 115
Burroughs, John, 112, 115, 127

C

Cambridge, 23
Canajoharie, 57, 58
Canajoharie Library and Art Gallery, 57 ,58
Canandaigua, 82, 84
Caramoor, 9–10
Casino (Saratoga), 31, 32
Cayuga Museum, 87, 88
Cazenovia, 68
Cazenovia Lake, 6
Champlain, Samuel de, 39
Champlain Canal, 53
Chautauqua, 100, 101
Chautauqua Institution, 100, 101
Church, Frederic Edwin, 18, 19
Children's Museum, 62, 63
Clayton, 44
Clemens, Samuel Langhorne (Mark Twain), 72, 73, 96, 126
Clermont (Livingston home), 16, 17
Clermont (Steamboat), 16
Cold Spring Harbor, 135, 136
Connetquot River Park, 139
Constitution Island, 106, 107
Cooper, James Fenimore, 14, 50, 59
Cooperstown, 59, 60
Corning, 74, 75
Coxsackie, 113
Crailo, 20, 21
Crailo Gardens, 16
Crown Point, 35, 36
Crown Point State Historic Site, 35, 36
Curtiss, Glenn H., 75, 76

D

Davis, Alexander Jackson, 5, 6
Deansboro, 64, 65
Delaware and Hudson Canal Museum, 111, 112
Durham Center Museum, 114

Index

Dyckman, States Morris, 11, 12
Dyckman House, 123

E
East Aurora, 103, 104
East Bloomfield, 81
East Durham, 114, 115
East Meredith, 115, 116
Eastman, George, 78, 79
Elbert Hubbard Museum, 103, 104
Electronic Communications Museum, 81, 82
Elmira, 72, 73, 74
Erie Canal, 50, 54, 55, 65, 66, 68, 92, 95
Erie Canal Museum, 68, 69
Erie Canal Village, 65, 66
Everson Museum of Art, 69, 70

F
Farmers' Museum, 59, 60
Fenimore House, 59, 60
Fillmore, Millard, 104
Finger Lakes Region, 72, 75, 76, 86, 88, 104
Fishers (town), 81
Fishkill, 12, 14
Fitzgerald, F. Scott, 96
Fonda, 56, 57
Fonda National Shrine of Blessed Kateri Tekakwitha, 56, 57
Fort Hunter, 55
Fort Klock Historic Restoration, 58, 59
Fort Niagara State Park, 94, 95
Fort Ontario State Historic Site, 45
Fort Ticonderoga, 34, 35
Frederic Remington Art Museum, 42, 43
Fulton, Robert, 17
Fulton County Museum, 57

G
Garrison-on-Hudson, 12
Genesee Country Village and Museum, 76, 77
Germantown, 16
Glenn H. Curtiss Museum, 75, 76
Glens Falls, 32, 33

Gloversville, 57
Goshen, 109
Gould, Jay, 7
Granger Homestead and Carriage Museum, 82

H
Hall of Fame of the Trotter and Trotting Horse Museum, 107, 108, 109
Hamilton, Alexander, 8, 52
Hammondsport, 75, 76
Hanford Mills Museum, 115, 116
Hempstead, 132
Herkimer, General Nicholas, 63, 64
High Falls, 110, 111, 112
High Rock Park Conservation Center, 130
Hill Cumorah, 84, 85
Historic Hudson Valley, 8
Historic Palmyra Museum, 85, 86
Hoffman Clock Museum, 86
Hubbard, Elbert, 102, 103
Hudson (town), 18, 19
Hudson River Museum, 2, 3
Huguenot Street, 109, 110, 111
Huntington, 136
Hyde Collection, 33, 34

I
Ilion, 61, 62
Iroquois Confederation, 39, 56
Iroquois National Wildlife Refuge, 92, 93
Irving, Washington, viii, 7, 8

J
Jacques Marchais Center of Tibetan Art, 128, 129
Jay, John, 8–9
Jogues, Isaac, S.J., 55, 56
John Brown Farm State Historic Site, 37, 38
John Jay Homestead, 8–9
Johnstown, 57

K
Katonah, 9–10

Kent-Delord House, 40, 41
Krebs, The (restaurant), 88, 89

L
Lake Placid, 37
la Salle, Robert Cavalier, Sieur de, 94
Lawrence, 132
Livingston, Robert, and Livingston Family, 16, 17
Lorenzo State Historic Site, 67, 68
Lyndhurst, 5, 7

M
Margaret Woodbury Strong Museum, 79, 80
Mark Twain Study, 72, 73
Massena, 42
McKim, Mead, and White, 14
McKinley, William, 96
Mechanicville, 27
Memorial Day Museum, 86, 87
Millard Fillmore House National Landmark, 104
Mills, Ogden, 14, 15
Mills Mansion, 14, 15
Monroe, James, 40
Montcalm, Marquis de, 34
Mt. Defiance, 35
Mt. Independence (Vermont), 35
Mt. Lebanon, 19
Mt. Marcy, 26
Mumford, 78
Munson Williams Proctor Institute, 62
Museum of Bronx History, 124
Museum of Cartoon Art, 5
Museum of the American Indian, 118, 120, *illus., 119*
Musical Museum, 64, 65

N
National Museum of Racing and Hall of Fame, 30, 31
National Shrine of the North American Martyrs, 56
National Soaring Museum, 73, 74
New Paltz, 109, 110
New Rochelle, 4, 5
New Skete Communities, 23
New York City, 118–141

Newark, NY, 86
North Chili, 78, 79
North Elba, 38
Northport, 137

O
Oak Orchard and Tonawanda Wildlife Management
  Areas, 92, 93
Oakdale, 140
Ogdensburg, 42, 43
Olana, 18, 19, *illus.,* 18
Old Bethpage, 138
Old Bethpage Village, 137, 138
Old Chatham, 19, 20
Old Fort Niagara, 94, 95
Old Rhinebeck Aerodrome, 15, 16
Olmsted, Frederick Law, 19, 140
Onchiota, 39
Oriskany, 64
Oriskany Battlefield State Historic Site, 63, 64
Oswego, 45, 46
Oyster Bay, 132, 134

P
Paine, Thomas, 4
Palmyra, 85, 86
Petrified Gardens, 32
Philipsburg Manor, 8
Philipse Manor Hall, 3, 4, 14
Phyfe, Duncan, 12
Planting Fields Arboretum, 133, 134
Plattsburgh, 40, 41
Poe, Edgar Allen, 124, 125
Poe Cottage, 124, 125
Putnam, Gen. Israel, 12

Q
Q-R-S Music Rolls, 98, 99
Queens, 126, 127

R
Remington, Eliphalet, 61
Remington, Frederic, 42, 43

Remington Firearms Museum, 61, 62
Remsen, 48
Rensselaer, 20, 21
Rensselaer County Junior Museum, 21, 22
Revere Factory Store, 66, 67
Rhinebeck, 15
Richmondtown Restoration, 129, 130
Richter's Butterfly Museum, 114, 115
Rochester, 79, 80
Rock Hall, 132
Rockwell Museum, 74, 75
Rome, 66
Roosevelt, Franklin, 30
Roosevelt, Theodore, 96, 97, 112, 121, 122
Rosen, Walter Tower & Lucie Dodge, 9, 10
Roxbury, 115
Roycroft Community, 103
Roycroft Campus, 103
Rye Brook, 5

S

Sackets Harbor, 45
Sackets Harbor Battlefield, 45
Sag Harbor, 45
Saint Johnsville, 58, 59
Saint Lawrence Seaway, 41, 42
St. Leger, Col. Barry, 27, 63, 64
Saranac Lake, 37, 39
Saratoga, Battle of, 27
Saratoga National Historical Park, 27, 29, *illus., 28*
Saratoga Spa State Park, 29, 30
Saratoga Springs, 30, 31, 32
Sargent, Charles Sprague, 140
Schapiro's (winery), 121
Schoharie Crossing State Historic Site, 54, 55
Schuyler Philip, and Schuyler Family, 51, 52
Schuyler Mansion State Historic Site, 51, 52
Seaford, 139
Shaker Museum, 19, 20
Shakers, vi
Six Nations Indian Museum, 39, 40
Skaneateles, 88, 89
Slabsides, 112

Smith, Joseph (and Mormonism), vi, 84, 85
Sonnenberg Gardens, 82, 83, 84
Southeast Museum, 10, 11
Staatsburg, 14, 15
Staten Island, 128, 129, 130, 131
Staten Island Institute of Arts and Sciences, 130, 131
Steuben Memorial State Historic Site, 46, 47, 48
Stillwater, 27, 29
Stuyvesant, Peter, 127
Suffolk Marine Museum, 140, 141
Sunnyside, 7–8
Syracuse, 69, 70

T
Tackapausha Museum and Preserve, 139
Tarrytown, 7
Tekakwitha, Kateri, 56
Theodore Roosevelt Birthplace National Historic Site, 121, 122
Theodore Roosevelt Inaugural National Historic Site, 96
Thomas Paine Cottage and Museum , 4, 5
Thousand Islands, 43
Thousand Islands Shipyard Museum, 44
Ticonderoga, 35
Tiffany, Louis Comfort, 140
Toscanini, Arturo, 126
Troy, 21, 22

U
Utica, 62, 63

V
Valentown Museum, 80, 81
Van Cortlandt Manor, 8
Van Rensselaer Family, 21
Van Wyck Homestead, 12, 13
Victorian Doll Museum, 78, 79
Village Blacksmith, 136, 137
von Steuben, Frederick, 46, 47, 48

W
Wagner College Planetarium, 131
Walloomsac, 22
Walt Whitman Birthplace, 136

Index

Washington, George, 14, 47, 52, 106
Waterford, 52, 53
Waterford Flight, 53
Waterford Historical Museum and Cultural Center, 53
Waterloo, 86, 87
Wave Hill, 125, 126
West Park, 112
West Point, 106, 107
West Sayville, 141
Whaling Museum, 135, 136
Whitman, Walt, 136
William Phelps General Store Museum, 86
William T. Davis Wildlife Refuge, 130
Wine and Grape Museum of Greyton H. Taylor, 76
Wright, Frank Lloyd, 97, 98
Wurtsboro, 109
Wurstboro Airport, 109

Y
Yonkers, 2
Young, Brigham, 85
Youngstown, 95

About the Author

William G. Scheller, contributing editor of *National Geographic Traveler,* is also the author of *New Jersey: Off the Beaten Path* and the Appalachian Mountain Club's *Country Walks Near New York.* His articles have appeared in the *Washington Post Magazine,* the *Christian Science Monitor,* and *Canoe.*